Trace
Your
Roots

Trace Your Roots

Published by:
Greatest Guides Limited, Woodstock, Bridge End, Warwick
CV34 6PD, United Kingdom

www.greatestguides.com

Every effort has been made to ensure that this book contains
accurate and current information. However, neither the author
nor the publisher shall be liable for any loss or damage suffered
by readers as a result of any information contained herein.

All trademarks are acknowledged as belonging to their
respective companies.

Greatest Guides is committed to a sustainable future for our
planet. This book is printed on paper certified by the Forest
Stewardship Council.

MIX
Paper
FSC   FSC® C020837

Printed and bound in the United Kingdom

ISBN 978-1-907906-11-4

To Ken and Elsie Kilminster,
the best parents I could have wished for.

Contents

Foreword

Never before has genealogy been as popular as it is today, but what is it that makes us so inquisitive? Perhaps it's a family legend of royalty connections, a secret linked to a notorious forebear, or simply a burning curiosity to know who we really are.

Whatever the reason, there are intriguing ancestors – and plenty of them – in everyone's family tree. Think of it like this: for every generation we go back, we double the number of our direct ancestors – two parents, four grandparents, eight great grandparents, and so on. By the time we reach the 16th century, we could each be looking for over one thousand people!

But, for me, genealogy isn't just about drawing up a pedigree with a long list of names that go back to the year dot. It's about widening our knowledge of the times our ancestors lived through, finding out what they did, and getting to know the sort of people they were. By doing this, we bring our own unique history to life.

In my role as a researcher, I've shared in people's joys and frustrations; had a great deal of fun, and met some wonderful people – and a few eccentrics – along the way! I've been asked to prove connections to several famous people in history, from British monarchs to pioneers of the American Wild West. But all of my clients have had one thing in common – a fascination for discovering their personal genealogy.

Everyone's family history is different. The tips in this book will show you the best tricks of the trade for finding your British ancestors; how to begin your research from scratch; what the most useful records are, and where to find them; what to do if you get stuck; and how to create your very own archive.

You're about to set off on a remarkable quest…

Good luck and happy hunting!

Maureen

Getting Back to the Old Country

" Generations pass like leaves fall from our family tree. Each season new life blossoms and grows benefiting from the strength and experience of those who went before. "

Heidi Swapp

Chapter 1
Getting Back to the Old Country

There are few things more satisfying than building your family tree – even if you do find a skeleton or two lingering in a closet! But what if your ancestor began life in the British Isles, how do you set about tracking them down? People left the old country for a variety of reasons – economic, religious, or to find a better life for themselves and their families. Then, of course, there were those who didn't leave by choice, but who were shipped out to the British colonies as convicts.

Many thousands of Americans, Canadians and Australians have a British family line, so the first section of this book takes a peek at some of the more useful resources to help track down where in the U.K. your pioneer ancestor originally came from.

ON YOUR MARKS, GET SET, STOP...

Utilize all the available resources in your home country to first establish where your family members originated. Many British records are kept in local repositories, making it vital that you discover your ancestors' exact location. England, Scotland, Wales and Ireland are divided into dozens of counties or regions, each comprising numerous towns and villages, with the main towns having a record office holding the local archives for that particular district.

MAILING LISTS

Before you travel the long road back to the 'old country', check out some online mailing lists. These could supply vital information about your ancestors by connecting you with folk who've already researched family lines that tie-in with your own.
http://lists.rootsweb.ancestry.com

MOVING THE BOUNDARIES

There is nothing the powers-that-be like better than to shift things around. The county boundaries of many places in the U.K. have been altered over the years, with towns first appearing in one county and then another, so do be aware of these anomalies when looking up your ancestor's place of origin.

FREE CHARTS ANYONE!

The lovely folk at the Ellis Island website will provide you with free, downloadable charts and forms, which are great for keeping a record of your discoveries. Charts include: Pedigree Chart, Family Group Sheet and Passenger Arrival Log.
http://www.ellisisland.org/genealogy/genealogy_charts.asp

SHIPS LISTS

The Ships Lists website has a zillion links for anyone interested in tracing their immigrant ancestors!
www.theshipslist.com

LINKS WITH IRELAND

And for your Irish immigrant ancestors, check out the Irish Times website.
http://www.irishtimes.com/ancestor/index.htm

STARTING POINT: UNITED STATES OF AMERICA

NATURALIZATION RECORDS

Sometimes naturalization papers can be more enlightening than searching through ship passenger lists. These records can highlight an immigrant's place of birth and previous address, along with the date of arrival in his adopted country.

It's not always easy to find all the documents that make up the naturalization procedure, but searching them out can often lead you to further important documents.

Do bear in mind that, during the colonial time period, your English ancestors, being British subjects already, won't show up in naturalization records. There may, however, be records of them in either England or in the colonies, if they originated from another European country and immigrated to Britain before moving on to the U.S.

KNOW YOUR ENEMY!

If your British ancestor was never naturalized then he should appear in the register of 'enemy aliens', even though it's possible he had lived (quite amiably!) in the U.S. for half his lifetime. This register was compiled during the War of 1812 and can be searched by state of residence.
Book: *British Aliens in the United States during the War of 1812* by Kenneth Scott

REPORTS OF BRITISH ALIENS

It was mandatory, from July 1812, for British aliens to fill out a report giving details of their families. These reports list useful things, such as the names of family members who were 14 years or older, how long they had been in the United States, their place of residence and their occupation.

Ancestry.com has a list that contains some 12,000 names of British aliens.
http://search.ancestry.com/search/db.aspx?dbid=49091

NATURALIZATION AND FEDERAL CENSUSES

Naturalization in the U.S. was not compulsory and so not everyone took the trouble. Check out the Federal censuses for 1820, 1830, 1870, 1900, 1910 and 1920 as they each have a section that indicates citizenship status, with the 1920 census giving the year when naturalization took place.

Note the abbreviations: AL, PA and NA in the citizen status area as these will tell you where your ancestor was at in the naturalization stakes.

- AL means that the person had not started down the naturalization route and was still an alien.

- PA means the person had begun the process and had filed his 'first papers'.

- NA means the process was complete and that he was a naturalized citizen.

USEFUL COURT RECORDS

People could become naturalized in many types of law court; often they chose a county court as being the one most conveniently situated to them. The naturalization records you seek may be held in one of these. Other courts might include: federal, district, chancery, circuit and some state supreme courts. Some records show up in state or local archives.

The National Archives have some records of naturalization that took place in federal courts, listed by state.
www.archives.gov/locations/index.html

There is a list of State Archives on the National Archives website where you can request a search for the state, county, and local court records where the naturalization took place.
www.archives.gov/research/alic/reference/state-archives.html

KEEPING IT OFFICIAL

From 1906, it was a requirement that a record of naturalization proceedings be noted by the clerk of the court and a copy forwarded to a central office – now the U.S. Citizenship and Immigration Services.
www.uscis.gov

DECLARATION OF INTENT

Also known as the 'first papers', the Declaration of Intent (DI) was filed by an alien after living in the U.S. for two years – the full procedure of naturalization taking a minimum of five years. The DI document can often point at the date of your ancestor's immigration and it will sometimes give the name of the ship on which he traveled.

CERTIFICATE OF CITIZENSHIP

The petition, or 'final papers', was generally issued three years after the Declaration of Intent and can be a useful way of furthering your research. Before being issued with a certificate of citizenship (the final part of the process), your ancestor was required to take along witnesses to testify on his behalf and these were quite often other relatives. The names and addresses of these witnesses are generally on record.

AUTOMATIC CITIZENSHIP FOR SOME

Not everyone had to file papers; for some, U.S. citizenship was an automatic process. This applied to:

- Wives of naturalized men (from 1790 to 1922).

- An alien woman who married a U.S. citizen.

- Children under 21 years – when their fathers became naturalized citizens (from 1790 to 1940).

Sadly, for family history historians, it is rare indeed to find names or other information about wives and children on DI or petitions prior to 1906.

EXCEPTIONS FOR WAR VETERANS

Certain other rules, concerning war veterans, come into play when considering U.S. citizenship:

- A new law in 1862 meant army veterans of any war, who had been honorably discharged, could apply after residing for just one year in the country.

- Similarly, a law in 1894 allowed honorably discharged five-year veterans of the navy or marine corps to petition for naturalization without filing 'first papers'.

- After 1918, aliens who served in the U.S. armed forces during the First World War were granted the right to petition for naturalization without the usual five-year residence or filing 'first papers'.

A FEW FURTHER POINTS...

Your ancestor may have filed in one court but completed the procedure someplace else entirely, so the 'first papers' and the 'final papers' will be found in separate locations.

The truth, the whole truth, and nothing but the truth might not always have been the case either. To shorten the waiting time, some people may have been tempted to give an inaccurate arrival date.

Some incorrect answers were inevitably supplied – unknowingly of course.

Not every immigrant who began the naturalization process would have completed it.

PASSPORTS TO SUCCESS!

Beginning in the year 1795, passport applications can be a helpful resource when tracing immigrant ancestors. The originals (prior to 1925) are held at the National Archives.
www.archives.gov/research/passport/index.html

They are also on microfilm at the Family History Library in Salt Lake City.
www.familysearch.org

You can request passport records, on payment of a fee, for owners who were born more than 100 years ago:
http://travel.state.gov/passport/npic/npic_872.html

PASSPORT EXTRAS

A passport application will show the names, ages and relationship to the applicant, of other people who accompanied him or her on their travels. These could be a wife, children, or servants on a male's application, or children who were to accompany their mother.

AND FOR NATURALIZED CITIZENS...

A passport application may have some detail about when a person became a naturalized U.S. citizen. The records sometimes give the court and the date of naturalization, as well as the date and the name of the ship upon which the person immigrated to the country.

WHAT YOU CAN LEARN FROM THE PASSENGER LISTS

There are six vital bits of info to be gained from these lists after 1820:

- Name

- Sex

- Age

- Nationality

- Occupation

- Intended destination

The Passenger Act of 1882 meant the country of origin was also added to the list of requirements.

SHIP PASSENGER ARRIVAL RECORDS

The National Archives have records of immigrants arriving in the U.S. from 1820 to 1982, with a list of microfilm available, listed by port. **www.archives.gov/research/immigration/index.html**

THE ELLIS ISLAND ARCHIVES

Between 1892 and 1924, a staggering 25 million passengers and crew members passed through Ellis Island and the Port of New York. Each person's details were recorded in the ships' passenger lists and these can be searched in the Passenger Record Archive at Ellis Island. Data includes a person's name, age, arrival date and name of ship.

You may also gain some historic insight about the ship itself – possibly even a picture! **www.ellisisland.org**

CONNECTING FAMILY

When searching through the passenger lists, make a note of all those who share the same surname as the person you're looking for – these may not have any connection to your family, but they might just turn out to be related in some way.

WHERE AND WHEN?

Immigrants arrived in the U.S. via five main ports: New York, Boston, Philadelphia, New Orleans and Baltimore. Though New York was the most important port of entry for passengers from the British Isles, you might also try checking out the port indexes closest to where your ancestor made his home. If you hit the target, you'll discover the date of arrival and the name of the ship.

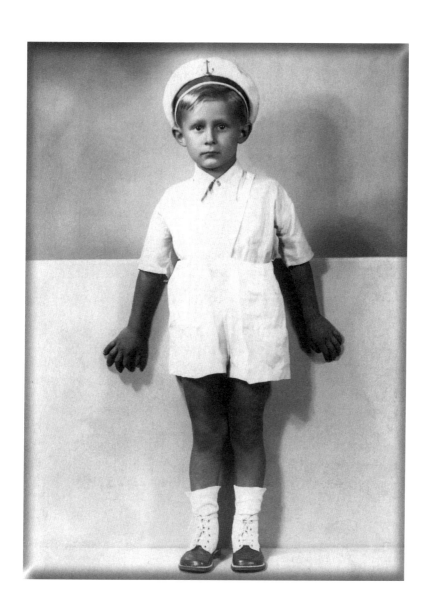

STARTING POINT: CANADA

NATURALIZATION

Up until 1947, there was no legal requirement for immigrants from England, Scotland, Wales or Ireland to naturalize, as those hailing from Great Britain were already considered citizens of Canada.

Some immigrants did apply and confirmation of this can be found in censuses and other documents, including passports, land records, military papers and voting registers.

The Library and Archives Canada has naturalization registers covering the years 1828 to 1850 for Upper Canada/Canada West (Ontario).
http://www.collectionscanada.gc.ca

Sadly, the records compiled for the whole of Canada, by the Department of the Secretary of State for the years 1865-1917, were destroyed. But there remains an index of names, place of residence and court certification; apply in writing to: Records Control
Citizenship Registration Branch
Department of the Secretary of State
P.O. Box 7000 Sydney, NS
B1P 6G5
Canada

CANADIAN CENSUSES

The census returns covering the years 1851, 1861, 1871, 1881, 1891, 1901, 1906, 1911 and 1916 will give the following information:

- Name

- Age

- Gender

- Marital status

- Religion

- Ethnic origin

- Country or province of birth

Of particular help to anyone hunting down their immigrant ancestors are the censuses of 1901 and 1911, as these include details of a person's year of immigration, as well as their date of birth.
http://landing.ancestry.ca/CACensus/en/default.aspx

NATIONAL REGISTRATION FROM 1940 TO 1946

The 1940 National Registration is a record of all adults in Canada. Originally compiled by the War Measures Act and the National Resources Mobilization Act, registration was compulsory for anyone aged 16 and over, but excluding members of the armed forces and a few other exceptions.

Along with basic information, like name, address, date of birth and occupation, there are fields that aid those researching immigrant ancestors, such as: nationality, year of entry into the country and racial origin.

Enquiries about these records can be made by contacting Statistics Canada:

Census Pension Searches Unit
Census Operations Division
Statistics Canada
B1E-34 Jean Talon Building
Tunney's Pasture
Ottawa, ON
K1A 0T6
Tel: 613-951-9483

PASSENGER LISTS PRE-1865

Prior to 1865, shipping companies were not obliged to keep a record of passengers, so details before this date are sketchy. But the Olive Tree Genealogy website has a number of indexes of passengers' names.
www.olivetreegenealogy.com

AFTER 1865

The passenger lists after this date, arranged by port and date of arrival, give info, such as name, age, occupation, place of origin and destination. The Records from the following ports are searchable on the Library and Archives Canada website.

Quebec (1865-1921)
Halifax (1881-1922)
Saint John (1900-1922)
North Sydney (1906-1922)
Vancouver (1905-1922)
Victoria (1905-1922)
New York (1906-1922)
Eastern American coast (1905-1922)
http://www.collectionscanada.gc.ca/databases/passenger/index-e.html

You can search Canadian passenger lists from 1865 to 1935 at Ancestry.ca
http://search.ancestry.ca/search/db.aspx?dbid=1263

SHIPPING SEASON

Quebec was where the vast majority of immigrants arrived in Canada. But, with the shipping season lasting 24 weeks, and the St. Lawrence River closed to shipping in winter, it's worth checking other ports, such as New York, Boston, Portland, Halifax and Saint John for family who arrived during the winter months.

PASSAGE TO CANADA

Try the online database of ships' passengers at The Library and Archives Canada if you're looking for family who arrived as immigrants in Canada between 1925 and 1935. Go through the 'Exploration and Settlement' link to 'Search Immigration Records from 1925-1935' in the Ancestors Search area of the site.
www.collectionscanada.ca

PASSENGER LISTS AFTER 1936

You can obtain a copy of another's immigration record for genealogical research purposes from Citizenship and Immigration Canada by submitting a request via an Access to Information form. You must be a Canadian citizen or reside in Canada and you need a proof of the person's death (it must have occurred at least 20 years ago), or a signed consent form from the person concerned.
www.cic.gc.ca

LAND RECORDS

If your ancestor was one of the many who submitted a petition for Crown Land, the land records could supply you with some interesting findings. These could include administration records, reports from the Surveyor General or the Attorney General, and requests for grants or leases.

FINDING THE RIGHT LAND RECORDS

Be sure you're looking in the right place when consulting the land records. Ontario was once part of Quebec (up until 1791) and Quebec and Ontario were once part of the United Province of Canada (from 1841 to 1867).

So, if you want the Ontario petitions prior to 1791, you'll need to consult the Lower Canada Land Petitions, and, for Quebec petitions after 1841, the Upper Canada Land Petitions. Easy, isn't it, when you know how!

Details of available land records can be found on the Library and Archives Canada website.

EXTRA FAMILY INFO

Some Ontario land petitions contain added bonuses for family historians. If your ancestor was a Loyalist or a discharged soldier, you might find that they've given their regiment. Other really helpful info comes by way of the sons and daughters of Loyalists, as they were apt to give their father's name, too. And, not to be outdone in the useful family history info stakes, civilian petitioners may well have mentioned their place of origin.
http://www.archives.gov.on.ca

LOYALISTS' CONNECTIONS

If your ancestor remained loyal to the British Crown, he may well have settled in what are now the provinces of Quebec, Ontario, Nova Scotia, New Brunswick and Prince Edward Island.

Quebec: www.banq.qc.ca
Ontario: www.archives.gov.on.ca
Nova Scotia: www.gov.ns.ca
New Brunswick: http://archives.gnb.ca
Prince Edward Island: http://www.gov.pe.ca/cca

HOME CHILDREN

The British Isles Family History Society of Greater Ottawa has a searchable Home Children database, with the names, ages, name of ship and year of arrival of over 100,000 British children who were sent to Canada during the child emigration movement between 1869 and 1930.
www.bifhsgo.ca/cpage.php

GENEALOGICAL SOCIETIES

Help may be at hand at one of the family history societies; they can offer practical guidance about local records and resources.

A list of Canadian family history societies can be obtained here:
http://www.collectionscanada.gc.ca/genealogy/022-801-e.html

LINKS TO EVERYTHING!

Genealogy Links Canada is a great jumping off point for family historians researching their Canadian lines.
www.genealogylinks.net/canada

STARTING POINT: AUSTRALIA

TRANSPORTATION

Beginning in the latter half of the 1700s, around 160,000 convicts were transported to a penal colony in Australia from England, and other parts of the British Empire, before the practice was finally abolished in 1868.

There is a database of registers on Ancestry.com.au, which has helpful info for all fleets, though not all of the information below is held for every record. Generally, you might learn:

- Convict's name

- The date of conviction

- Where convicted

- The length of the sentence

- Name of ship

- Departure date

- Name of the designated penal colony

www.ancestry.com.au

PRISONERS' PARTICULARS

Other very good sources from Ancestry.com.au give lists of prisoners. These records often contain: names, trades and physical descriptions, along with place and date of conviction, sentence and ship name. The Australian Convict Collection area of the website has a number of links, as well as several free indexes.

http://search.ancestry.com.au/search/grouplist.aspx?group=auconvicts

NOT JUST CONVICTS!

Many Britons, who weren't convicts, arrived in Australia during the 19th century, too. Your ancestor may have decided to make a new life for himself by way of an emigration scheme, or may have been a soldier or a government official who accompanied the convict fleets.

Immigration was pretty much unrestricted until the Commonwealth of Australia took control of the situation in 1922.

HOW WILL YOU KNOW?

There are a few ways to tell if a person was a convict:

- Census records might indicate this.

- A death certificate that states the person was 'a prisoner of the Crown'.

- A couple's marriage certificate could say that they were married with the permission of the Governor, which means that one or the other was a convict.

CONVICT ANCESTORS CAN BE FUN TOO!

Here's a little light relief for those searching their convict ancestors, as well as some very useful information.

www.convictcentral.com

FREE NEW SOUTH WALES CONVICT DATABASE

Some 80,000 English, Scottish, Welsh and Irish convicts were transported to New South Wales between 1788 and 1842. The State Archives has a free database, which includes around 120,000 entries, including: certificates of freedom, tickets of leave, tickets of exemption from government labor, tickets of emancipation and pardon, and convict bank accounts (!).
www.records.nsw.gov.au

WESTERN AUSTRALIA CONVICT RECORDS

There are all kinds of transportation documents held at the State Records Office of Western Australia. These include things like: convict lists and registers, good conduct reports, medical registers, leave registers, general duties, expirees and pardons.
www.sro.wa.gov.au

IMMIGRATION RECORDS NSW

The State Records for New South Wales has a number of shipping records for arrivals and departures from NSW up to 1922. There's a free searchable index on their website for arrivals on various ships and dates:

- Port Phillip – 1839 to 1851

- Sydney & Newcastle – 1844 to 1859

- Moreton Bay (Brisbane) – 1848 to 1859

- Sydney – 1860 to 1879

- Sydney – 1880 to 1896

www.records.nsw.gov.au

ASSISTED PASSENGERS

Those folk at the State Records for NSW really are helpful! Amongst other stuff, they have a free online index that contains around 9,000 names of immigrants who paid their own fare. The info you can glean here includes: name, age, ship and date of arrival.

ASSISTED PASSAGE TO QUEENSLAND

The Queensland State Archives holds the immigration records for those arriving in Queensland ports. These records, mostly for assisted passengers, will be made available as indexes on their website.
www.archives.qld.gov.au

VICTORIA IMMIGRATION RECORDS

The Public Records Office in Victoria has digitized records and online indexes of passenger lists, which include an index to the unassisted inward passenger lists to Victoria from 1852 to 1923 and the index to assisted British immigration from 1839 to 1871.
www.access.prov.vic.gov.au

WESTERN AUSTRALIA PASSENGER LISTS

You can consult the passenger lists in the Search Room at the State Records Office of Western Australia. These lists will usually give the passenger's name, age, profession, date of arrival, name of ship, port of embarkation and where bound.
www.sro.wa.gov.au/archive-collection/search-room

NATIONAL ARCHIVES

The National Archives have records that date from 1922. They have certain data online and you can also view original records in one of their reading rooms around the country. As well as Canberra, their reading rooms are in Sydney, Melbourne, Brisbane, Perth, Adelaide, Hobart and Darwin.
www.naa.gov.au

MAKING AUSTRALIA HOME

The National Archives have a project called 'Making Australia Home', which will be of particular interest to the descendants of the seven million people who migrated there in the 20th century. These records include things like name, date of birth, place of origin and other family members. If you're lucky, there might be a photograph, too.

CENSUS DETAILS

Here's a really helpful site that lists the surviving censuses and musters in the Australian colonies and states and where you can track them down. www.jaunay.com/auscensus.html

A variety of census links can be found on the Explore Genealogy website. www.exploregenealogy.co.uk/AustralianCensus.html

NATURALIZATION

Before 1949, British subjects automatically had rights as citizens and so didn't need to undergo the naturalization procedure.

The process was the responsibility of individual colonies and states up until 1903, when the Australian government took over. The records from this time are held by the National Archives of Australia.

A bride adopting her husband's surname became the custom in the 15th century.

CHAPTER SUMMARY

- Utilize available resources in your home country to establish where your immigrant ancestor originated.

- Check out the online mailing lists.

- Early nationalization records for British colonies won't show U.K. subjects.

- U.S. 'first papers' and 'final papers' may be held in different locations.

- Passenger lists can give vital data.

- Make notes of those who share the same surname when checking passenger lists.

- Census returns often give immigrant information.

- A petition for Crown Land can show place of origin.

- Several records indicate whether a person was a convict.

- Check out assisted passengers, too – not every British immigrant was a convict!

In the Beginning...

" Some people are your relatives but others are your ancestors, and you choose the ones you want to have as ancestors. You create yourself out of those values. "

Ralph Ellison

Chapter 2
In the Beginning...

Before you start searching further afield, gather together all the evidence you can from those nearest to you. No matter how trivial it may seem at first. Just remember that small clues can lead to great discoveries!

QUESTIONS, QUESTIONS

One thing is certain; not everyone in your family will share your enthusiasm for uncovering the past. In fact, it's probably true to say that some won't give a toss. Never let this fact deter you. Instead, put together a questionnaire and distribute it doggedly to any relatives you think might be able to help. If you need to mail your questionnaire, it's a good idea to enclose a S.A.E. – thus ensuring they have one less excuse not to reply! Here are my lucky seven questions:

1. Is there a family bible or any other family papers in your possession?

2. Do you have any old birth, marriage or death certificates?

3. Thinking back to your childhood, what older family members do you remember?

4. How were they related to you and to each other?

5. Have you photos of any of these people?

6. Do you know exactly where they lived?

7. What were their professions?

TEST THE WATERS

Two tips in one here! If you're very new to genealogy, my first tip is to start with the branch of the family you're most familiar with. My second tip is to check out a few things you already have information about, so you can get a good feel for how the various systems and documents work. Try starting with parents' or grandparents' birth or marriage records, or look up a grandparent or great grandparent on the 1901 or 1911 British census.

ON THE SPOT

It will really pay off if you can get a few of those distant cousins involved in your family history project. If they still live in the same part of the country your shared ancestors came from, they will have much easier access than you do to all those lovely records at the local County Archives!

FAMILIES ARE NOT JUST FOR CHRISTMAS

Don't you just love all those family gatherings? If your response to that question was in the negative, just think of the rich store of information you can tap into at these events. My tip is to carry your notebook to every wedding, anniversary party and other assorted family knees up!

BROADEN YOUR OUTLOOK

It's possible that some papers vital to your research weren't passed down through your direct family line and that Great Aunt Flossie may have been entrusted to preserve the dynasty's all-important memorabilia, rather than your own dear Granny. Widen your search to include more distant family members.

THOSE WERE THE DAYS!

They say it's good to talk, and it is – especially to older relatives. A person's short-term memory may begin to fade with age but often their earliest recollections are as sharp as ever – and a gentle prod can work wonders!

- What sort of home did they live in; what about the furniture, garden and the neighborhood?

- Get them to tell you about their childhood. Did they have a favorite toy and what games did they play?

- Find out all you can about social gatherings and important family events. Did they take vacations or observe certain religious festivals?

- Ask about their working life.

- Were they, or others in their family, members of a club or society?

PHOTO OPPORTUNITY…

For some unfathomable reason, just about everyone seems to have the odd photo or two of a complete stranger in their collection. Who are all these people, and what are they doing in your family album? Show these snaps to any family member you think might have an inkling of who these mystery people are. They could turn out to be an important link.

WHAT ARE THEY WEARING!

The clothes worn in old photos can tell you quite a lot – not just that your ancestors had no dress sense! Those casual snaps taken in 'work' clothes reveal something of a person's social status; while more formally posed ones, with them sporting the newest, trendy clobber, will be better at indicating the time period.

THE DATING GAME

A word of warning if you're trying to date an old photo by studying the sitter's clothes: not everybody wore the latest fashions, whether by necessity or design, so a certain style of dress or suit might have been worn for quite a long period. For older people especially, fashion was less important and the style of dress didn't change a whole lot over the years.

A FLASH OF INSPIRATION!

Formal studio photographs are often stamped with the name and address of the photographer, which can help you to date an old picture. Search in old U.K. trade directories to find when the studio was in business. The town where the studio was situated may be where your ancestor once lived, so it will be worth further investigation.

NOT JUST A PRETTY FACE…

Look at what's beyond the person in a photograph – the landmark, house, shop, park, and so on, are the things that will help you pinpoint where the picture was taken. Ask other family members to help out if you don't recognize the places yourself.

CAUTION – FAMILY PEDIGREE AHEAD!

Should you come upon Great Uncle Walter's carefully drawn family tree lying in a shoebox at the bottom of a trunk behind a hat stand in the attic, try to curb your excitement until you've begun to check its legitimacy. Unlike today, when we have so many records easily and freely available to us, there was a time when people quite often compiled family pedigrees using little more than guesswork and rumor.

It wasn't too difficult to make the wrong assumptions; certain surnames are fairly commonplace in some areas, but are rare in others. It would have been easy enough to find that unusual name on a headstone, or inscribed on a church plaque, and have wrongly linked two unconnected families together. Likewise, there may well be several families in a village – and dozens in a town – who share a very common surname but who are unrelated.

Old Walter's pedigree could also be incomplete, showing only the male lineage with but a mere nod in the direction of the female family members – time for you to get better acquainted with the rest of your family and fill in all those blank spaces.

A BOX OF DELIGHTS!

Rummage in that ancient biscuit tin for a few treasures!

- Letters are normally dated and usually have the sender's address, as well as an address on the envelope. Apart from the letter's content, you can discover something about the recipient and family relationships by noting how the letter is worded – Dear Mrs, Dearest Aunt Maude, My darling, and so on.

- Long forgotten picture postcards could give you a useful address as well as a date (if you can make out the postmark).

- People often keep wedding invitations and these can be very useful to find. They'll supply you with dates, the names of the happy couple and where the marriage was to take place, along with some details of the bride's parents.

- Newspaper clippings are kept for all sorts of reasons, though, if you come upon a cutting for Mrs. Feelgood's Bear Grease Cure All, this might not be immediately relevant to your research! Make a note of any names you don't recognize. If the news item offers an important clue but the clipping isn't dated, search the newspaper archives to find the issue where it appeared.

DEAR DIARY

As personal documents go, they don't get much better than an old diary or journal. They can tell you a lot about your ancestor's personality and offer clues about what life was like for them. If you're lucky enough to find one, look for references to other people, and dates and locations where events took place. But remember that diaries and journals can be biased and give personal opinions rather than facts.

PASS IT ON…

There's something very special about a family heirloom, whether it's an emerald necklace or a treadle sewing machine! It can tell you a great deal about the life and times of the original owner and how this branch of the family tree fitted into the greater scheme of things. Somebody's favorite pastime, their taste, wealth or profession is revealed by what they chose to pass on to the next generation.

THOSE OLD SOUVENIRS

If one of your ancestors passed down a lot of souvenirs from a particular place, it suggests that they were frequent visitors. When vacations were rarer and traveling around the country wasn't simply a question of zipping off in the 4x4, that collection of 'Greetings from Bournemouth' knick-knacks may mean they lived fairly close or had other relatives in the area.

A FAMILY BIBLE

Families recorded the details of births, marriages and deaths in family Bibles long before civil registration began in the U.K., which gives you a head start in the genealogy race if you find one that has been passed down through your own family. Be sure to ask a wide circle of family members if such a book exists, as it could have ended up in the hands of what has now become a more distant branch of your family tree.

STICKING AROUND

If your U.K. ancestors were landowners, farmers, or had the sort of family business that passed from father to son, then I have good news for you. It should be a darn sight easier to track them down as it's likely the children won't have strayed too far from the fold (or Father's money), and you'll probably find the family living in the same parish for several generations. But while not every family stayed put in the same village or the same part of town, a great many didn't venture too far away either. If your trail goes cold in one parish, try looking in the adjoining ones first.

LEND AN ERA!

Most libraries stock a good selection of illustrated local history books, showing towns and villages, houses, businesses and transport. Use your library card and put your ancestors' lives into context by reading about a broader history of the district in the time period in which they lived. You could come across some local detail that aids your own research.

CREST FALLEN!

There are a lot of families who have the right to a coat of arms – though there are many more who don't! Be prepared to discover that the family crest embossed on Great Granny's silver teapot is, in fact, a fake, as the Victorians were taken-in big time. Well, let's face it, who could resist when faced with advertisements claiming to provide a genuine coat of arms to anyone who sent in their surname and place of origin? Check if the crest is authentic by submitting the details to the College of Arms.

Around 20 per cent
of Americans can
trace their ancestral roots
back to England, and
around 16 per cent
can trace theirs back
to Ireland.

CHAPTER SUMMARY

- Compile a questionnaire to distribute to family members.

- Research the branch of your family most familiar to you first.

- Learn how family history documents work.

- Take along a notebook to all family occasions.

- Talk to older relatives.

- Get in touch with more distant family members.

- Look at old family photographs.

- Beware unverified family pedigrees.

- Newspaper cuttings can offer vital clues.

- Check out local history books.

A Helping of Civil Sources

" We all grow up with the weight of history on us. Our ancestors dwell in the attics of our brains as they do in the spiraling chains of knowledge hidden in every cell of our bodies. "

Shirley Abbott

Chapter 3
A Helping of Civil Sources

Of course, nowadays our births, marriages and deaths are officially recorded, and these records are kept by the General Register Office (GRO), but, up until July 1837, there was no official registration in England and Wales. In Scotland, civil registration began in 1855 and, in Ireland, in 1864. If you're looking for earlier dates, the parish registers are what you need.

The other really helpful civil resource is the census – the population survey taken by the government every ten years. This began in 1801 and, although a few earlier censuses still exist, the 1841 is the first one that's any real help. Even with this one, things could be better! The census records have a certain closure period but you can look up lots of useful details about your ancestors from 1841 to 1911.

IT'S ALL IN THE TIMING

The GRO indexes are listed alphabetically by surname, but, to make things more interesting for you, they've arranged those lists in quarter years; March, June, September and December. If your ancestor was born, got married or died during January, February or March, then the event should have been registered in the March quarter, and so on. But this doesn't always follow.

- Events that actually took place towards the end of a quarter will likely not show up until the next quarter.

- A birth, marriage or death that took place in December of one year may not have been registered officially until the March quarter of the following year.

- Some people didn't register an event at all, especially in the years before 1875, when tougher measures were introduced.

INITIAL ERRORS

The GRO indexes are lists that have been transcribed from the original registrars' returns and, in some cases, may have been copied incorrectly or even misheard by the registrar in the first place. If you haven't turned up a surname in the index where you think it ought to be, have a go at substituting similar looking initial letters – C for G, M for N and P for R – Norris may have become Morris or Probert might be listed under Robert, for example.

Or try adding or taking away the letter H – it's possible that the registrar thought someone was 'dropping his aitches' and so wrongly 'corrected' Alford to Halford and so on.

NAME DROPPING!

A forename chosen by the parents and registered at birth may be different from the one by which that person was later known. This doesn't mean anything sinister and is more likely to be a case of the person disliking the name or changing it to avoid confusion when the child's father had the same handle!

Quite often, people swapped names around and used their middle one. If you've searched the GRO lists without luck, try using the person's other forename, if this is known to you; if you don't have this info, search by surname and take note of any entries where the middle name is the one familiar to you.

HOSPITAL VISITING

Women weren't always sent home from hospital a few minutes after giving birth! In the times when they were allowed to spend a week or two recovering from the ordeal of junior's arrival, it was common for a registrar to visit the hospital on a regular basis to record each child's birth. This can mean a birth will show up in the index of the district where the maternity hospital was situated, which may have been some distance from where the child's family actually came from.

MORE HOSPITAL DRAMA!

Your ancestor could have died in a hospital that wasn't in the same area in which he or she lived and so the death registration might not show up where you would expect to find it. If this happens, it's quite likely you'll find the death was registered where the hospital was located – perhaps miles from their home and possibly even in a surrounding county.

MARRIAGES: THE PERFECT MATCH…

In the GRO indexes, although they share the same reference number, couples' names are listed separately, so you need to search both names (in the same year and quarter) and then check that the reference numbers match. To make things easier, search the least common surname first.

FINDING A CHILD'S PARENTS

When looking for the marriage of a child's parents, work backwards from the child's birth or baptism. But don't give up too soon – the child could be the youngest of a very large family, with the marriage taking place 20 years before! If you still can't find the marriage, work forwards from the child's birth, the couple might have married after the child was born.

AND BY THE SAME TOKEN…

If you have trouble locating the birth of the eldest child of the family in the GRO indexes, try searching under the mother's maiden name.

SIX REALLY USEFUL THINGS ABOUT A DEATH CERTIFICATE...

Of course, it goes without saying that these notifications confirm a death, but take a look at a few of your ancestors' certificates and they might help you fill in some valuable extra details – and that's always a good thing.

1. The certificate will give you the actual date of death, rather than the burial date found in a parish register.

2. You'll find out the place he or she died. This might not be where you thought, but may instead give you some, yet unexplored, avenues to follow.

3. It will state the age at death, though this might not always be accurate if the informant didn't know the person well.

4. The person's rank or profession is also given, which could open up some new areas of research.

5. It'll give the cause of death. If this was an accident, such events are often recorded in a local newspaper. It could also suggest an occupational hazard or an epidemic.

6. The informant's details are listed, including name, address and relationship to the deceased person. Registering a death was normally the task of the next of kin, so it's worth checking these names out – a woman informant who has a different surname might be a married daughter or sister, for instance.

SAVE TIME AND MONEY BY APPLYING DIRECT

Once you've found your ancestor's birth or death in the GRO indexes, it's quicker and cheaper to send for a copy of the certificate from the register office where the event was originally registered, rather than from the General Register Office. There's a list of addresses and contact details for England and Wales at:
www.ukbmd.org.uk/genuki/reg

A list of registration districts for Scotland can be found on the GRO for Scotland website:
www.gro-scotland.gov.uk

Information regarding Irish State Registration of Births, Marriages and Deaths is at:
www.irishtimes.com

Supply any information you know to be correct. Make your payment out to the Superintendent Registrar and ask that they issue the certificate only if it corresponds with the information you've supplied – that way you'll get your money returned if the details don't match! For a birth, it's useful if you can tell them:

■ The year and quarter in which the event is listed in the indexes.

■ The child's name.

■ Father's name, if known.

■ Mother's maiden name, if known.

■ The parish in which they lived.

BUT A MARRIAGE MIGHT TAKE LONGER...

You'll be on a hiding to nothing if you ask a registrar for a marriage certificate when you've no idea where the wedding took place. Unless you can supply him with this info, you're backing a loser here as, with no parish index, the registrar might have to search the registers of every church and chapel in his district before coming upon the one you want. Much less hassle to apply direct to the GRO!

BRITISH BIRTHS, MARRIAGES AND DEATHS AT SEA

Contact the National Archives if you're looking for details about an ancestor who was born, married or died at sea or abroad ship between 1831 and 1958. They hold the civil registration for these events, known as the (this will just roll off your tongue) Registrar General's Miscellaneous Non-statutory Foreign Returns.

WHERE CAN YOU SEE THE CENSUS RECORDS FOR FREE?

The census returns from 1841 to 1911 for England, Wales, the Channel Islands and the Isle of Man can be accessed online at:
www.nationalarchives.gov.uk/census

The National Archives provides free access to this service in its reading rooms, but there is a standard onsite charge for printing copies.

The Family Search website has a free searchable database for the 1881 British census.

County Archives and local reference libraries hold copies of the censuses for their own district on microform.

SIX HELPFUL THINGS YOU CAN GLEAN FROM A CENSUS RETURN…

1. The name or number of the house and the street your ancestor lived in.

2. Who the head of the household was.

3. A list of all the people who were in the house and how they were related to the householder.

4. Their ages and marital status.

5. Their occupations.

6. Their place of birth.

CENSUS OR NONSENSE!

Each census covered the period from Sunday night to Monday morning and every household was required to fill out a form. The completed form gave details of who was in the household during this time and was collected the following day by the enumerator, who then transcribed the information into another book. Sounds simply enough you might think, but things didn't always go according to plan. Watch out for mistakes due to:

- The instructions on the forms not being fully understood.

- People not able to spell.

- The enumerator wrongly transcribing what someone had written.

CARRY ON SEARCHING

When using the census returns, if you track down the ancestor you've been searching for in a particular district, don't stop looking! Note any entries of the same surname in that location as they might turn out to be related, especially if it isn't a common name.

AGE CONCERNS!

It may look like it, but people weren't necessarily lying about their ages on the 1841 census. Children under the age of 15 had to have their exact age listed, but anyone older had his or her age rounded down to the nearest five, so you must allow for certain anomalies. For example, if a woman was 24 then she would be recorded as 20, even though she married at 16 and has an eight year old child!

BUT DON'T RULE OUT FIBBING ALTOGETHER...

From 1851, all ages were meant to be given accurately, but people could have had their reasons for telling a few porkies!

- A person might have pretended they were younger if they felt their job was at risk if their employer knew the truth.

- Someone under 21 might say they were older in order to rent property.

- People were proud to reach old age so someone quite elderly may have really tried to impress by adding on a few extra years!

OR A LITTLE FORGETFULNESS…

Once you've discounted silly census rules and deliberate economies of truth, you can put down most inconsistencies in your ancestors' ages – when compared with an earlier or later census – to poor memory. People forget their own ages, and the ages of their spouses and children, all the time – so nothing new here! And maybe someone filling in the details on behalf of an elderly relative wouldn't have known their age.

SOME FINAL THOUGHTS ON AGES!

Remember that the census wasn't taken on the same date each time, so any discrepancy might be accounted for by your ancestor having celebrated a birthday during these weeks.

- 1841 – 6th June

- 1851 – 30th March

- 1861 – 7th April

- 1871 – 2nd April

- 1881 – 3rd April

- 1891 – 5th April

- 1901 – 31st March

- 1911 – 2nd April

By 1852, burials at most urban churchyards were forbidden for public health reasons, and new burial grounds, set up by local councils and private companies, were put in place.

JUMPING TO CONCLUSIONS

Unlike the later censuses, the 1841 doesn't show the relationship of each individual to the head of the household and, sometimes, identifying who's who in this census will be purely guesswork on your part! A man and woman living at the same address and who share the same surname could be man and wife, but they might also be brother and sister or father and daughter.

FARMER FOREBEARS

If your ancestor was a farmer, you'll get some added data for your family history file from the censuses that were taken between 1851 and 1881. During these dates, the farm acreages were also specified on the returns and also whether someone was an employer or an employee.

CONTEMPLATING NAVAL CENSUSES

British naval and merchant vessels, both at sea and in port, were included in the census returns from 1861. These are certainly worth looking into, though, unfortunately, they're not complete.

HOW BIG WAS YOUR ANCESTOR'S HOME?

You can fill in all sorts of riveting details about your ancestor's life from the census forms they completed. For instance, you'll know whether their living accommodation had fewer than five rooms, as this information had to be included on the census returns from 1891.

SURNAME SPELLING SLIP-UPS

When all the other data matches up, don't discard a census entry just because the surname isn't spelt the way you think it should be. There are several reasons why spellings differ; the census enumerator could have misread what was written on the form, or your family may have once used another spelling. And if you're using a census index, an error could have occurred during the indexing process.

NICKNAME NIGHTMARE!

The nickname your ancestor was known by to family and friends may have been given in the census records, rather than their proper name, so you might need to do a little lateral thinking to sort them out. Here are 10 popular names and their commonly-used nicknames.

1. Bella, Betsy, Lisa = Elizabeth

2. Daisy, Meg, Peggy = Margaret

3. Dodie, Dolly, Dora = Dorothy

4. Hettie = Esther

5. Jack = John

6. Jenny = Jane

7. Kate, Kitty = Katherine

8. Molly, Polly = Mary

9. Sadie, Sally = Sarah

10. Nell, Nora = Eleanor

FOUR WAYS TO CHECK IF THE PLACE OF BIRTH IS CORRECT

From 1851, the place of birth was included on the census; but not everyone got this right, which can mean locating a baptism record gets a bit tricky! The information given by parents about their child's place of birth is usually correct, but an older person may have mistakenly given the place where they grew up, rather than where they were born. Here are four top tips to help you track down your ancestor's place of birth.

1. The birth certificate will give the parents' address.

2. Look at a sibling's census entry to see the place of birth they've given.

3. If you have either parent's census details, try searching records from their parishes.

4. Check later censuses. Your ancestor may have given different information at a later date.

SOMEONE'S MISSING FROM THE FAMILY GROUP...

If a member of the family hasn't been included on the census form, but you're pretty certain they hadn't left home permanently at this time, look for them on the census entries of other close relatives, where they may have been visiting.

A TIP FOR WHEN YOU DON'T KNOW A WOMAN'S MARRIED NAME

This can be time consuming and works best if the woman in question had a not-too-common forename or, if you can consult an index for a particular area, limit the search results. Investigate any females who might be within the correct age range by searching her first name only. Once you have a list of promising ones, check where each was born to (hopefully) find a match!

SEARCH THE WORKHOUSE CENSUS

The census included workhouse inmates, so don't forget to search these if you're missing some ancestors. After 1834, couples were split up on entering the workhouse, so you'll need to check both the male and female listings to find a complete family.

SPOTTING AN ILLEGITIMATE CHILD ON THE CENSUS

It isn't always possible to spot an illegitimate child, but here are a few things to look out for:

- A child who retains his or her mother's maiden name.
- A child's name at the bottom of the family list and out of age sequence.
- A child who is referred to as 'wife's son or daughter'.

CHAPTER SUMMARY

- There is no civil record of births, marriages or deaths before 1837.

- You might need to search the GRO indexes beyond your 'known' dates.

- Check names using a variety of different spellings.

- The informant on a death certificate could prove to be a valuable lead.

- Birth and death certificates are cheaper from the local register offices.

- Local archives and libraries hold censuses for their own district.

- From 1851, the place of birth is shown on the census returns.

- Ages on the census aren't always correct.

- People sometimes used nicknames on the census.

- Remember to check the workhouse census.

Perusing the Parish Records

" The lives of great men all remind us, we can make our lives sublime, and, departing, leave behind us, footprints on the sands of time. "

Henry Wadsworth Longfellow

Chapter 4
Perusing the Parish Records

Amongst other things, the U.K. parish records include the church registers, which are the documents you need when tracing your family tree beyond 1837. In England and Wales, some parish registers date back to 1538, in Scotland to 1558 and in Ireland to 1634. Remember, though, that the parish registers record the dates of baptisms and burials rather than the births and deaths found in the civil registration lists.

A SECOND OPINION

Some old parish registers are in a very sorry state, with damaged and discolored pages or with entries looking, for all the world, like they were written using invisible ink. It's really just a matter of luck whether the registers you will need to consult were written by the vicar, who prided himself on his neat columns, or by the one who over-zealously filled every available space with an illegible scrawl!

Luckily, from the late 16th century, copies of the register entries were sent in annually to the diocesan registrar. These copies are called the Bishop's Transcripts and are usually held at County Archives. They're sometimes in a better condition than the parish registers, so my tip is to use these to verify information that is difficult to read in the registers.

SEEING DOUBLE!

If your ancestors appear to be baptizing two children with the same name within the space of a few years, don't panic, you're probably not seeing things. Quite often, when a child died, a new baby was given the same name. If you come across one of these repeated baptisms in your research, always look for an entry in the burial register for the first child.

FAMILY BAPTISMS

You might not always find a baptism where you'd expect to find it. If you have difficulty locating one, search further into the register before throwing in the towel, as some families had their entire brood baptized as a job lot!

BAPTIZING ILLEGITIMATE CHILDREN

These baptisms are easy enough to spot as they generally record the mother's name only. But the word the clergy used to describe the child's circumstances varies quite a lot. Look for any of these:

- Illegitimate

- Base

- Baseborn

- Bastard

- Spurious

- Supposed

- Misbegotten

IS HE THE FATHER OR ISN'T HE?

'Reputed' and 'imputed' are a couple of words that crop up from time to time in a baptism register. Something like: "Mary the reputed daughter of James Fletcher by Ann Jones" will tell you that James has admitted paternity. But if 'imputed' is used, it means everyone's pretty certain James is the father, but he's owned up to nothing!

SOMETIMES DAD'S NAME IS HANDED TO YOU ON A PLATE!

Occasionally, tracing the father of an illegitimate child isn't all that difficult. His name may conveniently appear in the baptism register, as in, "Mary Jones, daughter of Ann Jones and James Fletcher".

A child given two surnames in the baptism register is also a clue worth following: "Mary Fletcher Jones, daughter of Ann Jones".

MORE INFO IN PARISH REGISTERS AFTER 1813

Some bright spark in the early 19th century came up with a pretty smart idea because, after 1813, parish registers were produced complete with pre-printed pages. This enabled more information to be included as a matter of course, so a baptism entry will give you not only the parents' names but the area in which they lived (later their full address) and the father's occupation. It's also quite common to find the child's date of birth squeezed into the later entries.

MARRIAGE RULES OK!

Certain new rules were brought in, affecting marriages after 1754, which makes life a lot easier for family historians.

1. Marriages must be preceded by the calling of banns or by the issuing of a marriage license.

2. A record should be kept in an appropriate book.

3. Entries in the book should be signed by the couple and by witnesses to the marriage.

4. The ceremony must take place in the parish where the bride or groom reside.

The ancient custom of newly weds drinking a beverage of diluted honey during their first month of marriage, led to the word 'honeymoon'.

MARRIED BY BANNS

If you have trouble finding a marriage in the parish register, try searching the banns books. The banns are a public announcement of a forthcoming marriage and are announced in church on three Sundays preceding a marriage. If the marriage doesn't take place within three months of the last announcement, the process begins all over again.

MARRIED BY LICENSE

Copies of marriage licenses can often be found in County Archives. A couple may have obtained a license rather than have banns read out in church, if they wanted to marry in a hurry, or if they didn't want the parish gossips to know their business! A marriage license required two bondsmen to stand as guarantors and these were usually relatives.

CIVIL MARRIAGES

Marriages solely by license or banns continued until 1836, after which couples could marry in a civil ceremony conducted by a registrar. If you can't locate a marriage in the parish registers, try looking up the entry in the General Register Office indexes – a copy of the actual marriage certificate will indicate where the wedding took place.

DID YOU KNOW?

After 1837, a photocopy of the marriage entry in the parish register is as good as having a copy of the marriage certificate – and a lot cheaper. What you'll learn is:

- The couple's full names and addresses.

- Their ages – earlier entries may just say 'of full age'.

- Their occupations.

- Their fathers' names and occupations.

WITNESSES, CLUES AND DETECTIVE WORK

The parish register entry, or the marriage certificate, will also give you the names of two people who witnessed the marriage. As these witnesses were often related to the happy couple, they can throw up some valuable clues for further research; perhaps a married sister's new surname or the name of a brother's wife.

SO WHO'S COUNTING!

You may have to be a little flexible when it comes to noting down a bride's age; in some of the marriage records, she wasn't always as accurate as she ought to have been – after all, knocking a few years off is a bride's prerogative!

WHERE DID THEY BURY HIM?

There's always the odd ancestor who's never where you expect him to be! If you can't find his burial in the parish he died in, try the one where he was born – he may have wanted to be laid to rest near other members of his family.

NATIONAL BURIAL INDEX (NBI)

The Federation of Family History Societies is in the process of collating an index of burial records. To date, the extracts contain over 18 million records taken from Anglican parish, non-conformist, Quaker, Roman Catholic and cemetery burial registers in England and Wales. The NBI is sold on CD-ROM but most County Archive offices and some reference libraries have copies you can consult free of charge.

A POSSIBLE INDICATION OF A NON-CONFORMIST WEDDING

Non-conformists (or dissenters) were all those who followed a religion other than the Church of England. Between 1754 and 1837, only marriage ceremonies in the Anglican Church were legal – with Jews and Quaker marriages being the exception.

This isn't a foolproof system, but if you find a couple marrying by license in their local church, and then find no christening for the couple's children in the parish register, it could mean they were non-conformists.

A NON-CONFORMIST BAPTISM

The keepers of the non-conformist chapel books often gave more detail about those who were baptized than the parish clerk did in his registers. As well as the usual date, names, place of residence (and, later, the father's occupation), the chapel books often give the mother's maiden name and the child's date of birth.

NON-CONFORMIST BURIAL ENTRIES

As with the baptisms, the non-conformist burial register entries tend to supply some very useful extra pickings! Together with the date, name of deceased, and their last address and occupation, both parents' names are often listed when a child is buried. On a married woman's entry, her husband's name is sometimes given.

BURIED IN THE LOCAL CHURCHYARD

Check the parish church register, too. Not every non-conformist sect had a burial ground of its own, so members were buried in a part of the local churchyard. My tip is to look for a change in the way the clerk normally wrote up the burial entry in the parish register; he might have described the poor soul's laying to rest as, 'interred' or, possibly, 'hurled'!

LATER NON-CONFORMIST BURIALS

The burial of a non-conformist from around 1850 often took place in the unconsecrated part of a cemetery, which was run by a local burial board, rather than in a churchyard.

PARISH BURIAL REGISTERS OR INTERMENT REGISTERS – SPOT THE DIFFERENCE!

The parish churches keep registers to record the details of funerals that take place in the church. But whether or not a funeral was conducted in church, the cemetery where a person is laid to rest also holds a register of the interments. These cemeteries are usually run by district councils.

DISTANT DISSENTERS

Not all areas had their own non-conformist chapel, so, if your ancestors were dissenters, they may have had to trudge miles to attend the nearest meeting of their chosen sect. Be prepared to circle a wide area from where they lived to find any details about them.

WHO HOLDS THE RECORDS?

Some non-conformist registers were never handed in centrally and may still be languishing somewhere within the relevant chapel. County Archives hold a number of non-Anglican registers and they should be able to advise you on the whereabouts of others.

IRREGULAR MARRIAGES IN SCOTLAND

Church marriage registers in Scotland generally contain the proclamation of banns only. Irregular marriages (where no banns were called) could come about by a promise made in public, mutual consent, or by cohabitation with habit and repute. A list of custodians and owners of all the known existing records of Scottish irregular marriages is displayed on the General Register Office for Scotland website.
www.gro-scotland.gov.uk/famrec/sumrmar.html

QUAKER RECORDS

The minute books kept by the Religious Society of Friends (Quakers) records births, marriages, deaths and burials and you can consult those up to 1841 at the National Archives, and similar records up to 1837 by contacting the Society in London.

Births: Date and place of birth, the child's and parents' names (and, very useful this, occasionally the grandparents' names) and the father's occupation.

Marriage: Date, the couple's names and addresses, the man's occupation, the names and addresses of the couple's fathers, and a list of their relations and other friends who witnessed the happy event.

Death and burial: Date, name and address, age, occupation and, quite often, the deceased's parents.

THE ECCLESIASTICAL CENSUS

This tip is useful for locating a non-conformist chapel. In 1851, a country-wide census was taken of all places of worship. The census, arranged by county, was to include the address of every church, chapel or meeting house, the date each was built or founded, and the size of the congregation. The bad news is, the census isn't always complete for each district, but it's worth searching the County Archive copies.

DO YOU KEN YOUR SCOTTISH KIN?

Children in Scotland were named according to certain customs. Here's my tip to help you identify those Scottish ancestors.

- The first son was named after his paternal grandfather.

- The second son, after his maternal grandfather.

- The third son got his own father's name.

- The first daughter was named after her maternal grandmother.

- The second daughter, after her paternal grandmother.

- The third daughter got her own mother's name.

WELSH NAMING TRADITIONS

You'll find that surnames follow a different pattern in the earlier Welsh parish registers and this can be summed up in one word 'patronymics'; (it can be summed up in two words if you're counting the word 'confusing'). Instead of a fixed surname, each person was given their father's forename as their surname. For example: Thomas Morgan might be the son of Morgan Rees and Morgan Rees, the son of Rees Griffith.

ALL CHANGE – OR NOT…

The changeover from patronymics to fixed surnames took place from the early 1700s to the mid 1800s, with the decision to abandon the old system often dependant on how close they lived to their English neighbors. Not only that, but some Welsh clergy continued to record details in the parish registers using patronymics, even when the families had stopped! So, if you can't find an entry using the surname, try again using the patronymic name.

JOINED TOGETHER – DIFFERENT NAMES!

Another thing that often crops up in the older Welsh parish records is the practice of referring to a married woman by her maiden name, so don't let it throw you if, for example, you come across: Margaret Lewis, the wife of William Rees.

DON'T CONFUSE YOUR IN-LAWS WITH YOUR STEPS!

We all know the difference between a stepmother and a mother-in-law – there aren't so many jokes about stepmothers for one thing! But up until the early 19th century, the term 'in-law' was used for both, so this is something you might need to bear in mind when sorting out family relationships.

THREE REASONS WHY A CHILD MIGHT HAVE AN ALIAS

Some children are listed with aliases (James Smith alias Jones) and this can usually be accounted for in one of three ways:

1. The child is illegitimate.

2. The parents' marriage took place in a non-conformist chapel.

3. A widow remarried and the child is part of a stepfamily.

CHAPTER SUMMARY

- Use the Bishop's Transcripts when the parish registers are hard to read.

- Couples married in a parish where one of them resided.

- A marriage license lists two guarantors – often other family members.

- A burial may be in an ancestor's place of birth, not where they died.

- Check Anglican parish registers for non-conformist burials.

- Cemeteries have separate interment registers.

- Locate non-conformist chapels on the ecclesiastical census.

- Scottish naming customs mostly followed a particular pattern.

- Familiarize yourself with Welsh patronymic naming.

- Stepfamily members were once called 'in-laws'.

Delving into the Archives

" Some family trees have beautiful leaves, and some have just a bunch of nuts. Remember, it is the nuts that make the tree worth shaking. "

Anon

Chapter 5
Delving into the Archives

Did you know that The National Archives (NA) in Kew, Surrey (originally called The Public Record Office), houses all government records over a certain age and holds the largest collection of information about individuals and households during the 19th century?
www.nationalarchives.gov.uk/

County Archives (still sometimes known as a record office) hold records for that particular county and is where you'll find the parish registers and census returns. The huge variety of records held at these local archives means you'll be spoilt for choice, and they include things like wills and probate records, old newspapers and journals, Quarter Sessions records, Poor Law records, non-conformist registers, tithe maps, electoral registers and manorial records.

Local reference libraries also hold some genealogical gems; maps, censuses, newspapers and lots of other useful documents.

BE PREPARED

If you're planning a trip to The National Archives, here are a few tips worth knowing before your visit:

1. You'll be issued with a reader's ticket for looking at original documents, so remember to take some ID with you – a U.K. driving license, credit card, checkbook or passport are all acceptable.

2. Take a notebook or ring binder. You're allowed to take up to 20 loose sheets of paper into the reading rooms.

3. Equip yourself with pencils, as pens are not allowed.

4. No colored pencils or erasers.

5. Some areas of the reading rooms have points for laptops.

6. Digital photography is allowed in some areas, though flash photography is forbidden.

7. Cell phones must be turned to silent mode, but may be used to send text messages and to take photographs.

THREE THINGS TO DO – BEFORE YOU VISIT KEW

The sheer volume and range of material held at the NA is mind-boggling, so, to make sure you don't come out of there feeling you know less than when you went in, use this checklist before your visit:

- Write down what you already know and what you want to explore further.

- Check the online catalog to see what records might be relevant to you and the sort of information they contain.

- Make a list of the documents you think will help you and copy down their location and reference numbers.

ORDER DOCUMENTS IN ADVANCE

Save time and order documents before you visit The National Archives. Choose what you want from the online catalog and order the documents using the 'Request this' facility, or give them a ring. The documents will be produced the same day, if the request is made during document ordering hours.

There are more
than ten million
original documents
in the care of The
National Archives.

ANOTHER TIME-SAVING TIP

The NA allows you to view a maximum of 21 items a day. Because it can take anything up to 45 minutes to produce documents for each searcher, it's a really good idea to order up several at the same time – usually you're allowed to request three in one go.

COMING TO A FAMILY HISTORY CENTRE NEAR YOU!

If you can't get to the National Archives in Kew, all may not be lost. A lot of their records are available on microfilm and microfiche and you can hire them in at a Family History Centre, paying a small monthly or quarterly fee. These Centers are run by members of the Church of Jesus Christ of Latter-day Saints, so check their website to see if there's one near you!
www.familysearch.org

THE NATIONAL LIBRARY OF WALES

The NLW is the archive center for researching your Welsh genealogy. The collections include thousands of documents, photographs and pictures, maps and sound recordings. The resources are available free of charge but you'll need a reader's ticket to access the Reading Rooms. You need to take two proofs of identity, at least one showing your present address. Your photograph will be taken and printed onto your reader's ticket and a copy kept by NLW for security purposes. There's an application form on their website at:
www.llgc.org.uk

WEB CHECKS

It's practically unheard of now for a County Archives office or a library not to have a website. So before you spend time and money traveling to these places, check online for any descriptions of the records they hold, their policies regarding access or restrictions to documents, and any charges they make. Opening times, telephone numbers, email addresses and a location map are usually included, too.

HOW TO AVOID THE 'LOST SHEEP' LOOK

County Archives usually produce their own information leaflets, so request these before your visit. The leaflets give a general overview of what records are available and how the particular system works at each office. They'll often include a plan of the reading room, so you'll already have a fair idea of where various documents are kept before you get there.

PICTURE THIS…

Collections of original photographs and old picture postcards are held in County Archives and reference libraries. See if they have anything that might be connected to your own research – village scenes are particularly useful and may show your ancestor's home, or even your ancestor!

UPSTAIRS, DOWNSTAIRS, IN THE COUNTY ARCHIVES!

Large households usually meant domestic servants, and a record of wages paid to these people would have been kept in an account book. Many of these household inventories have been deposited in local archives, so these are worth looking out for if your ancestor was someone who worked 'below stairs' as a butler, cook, maid, coachman or gardener.

DIRECTORY ENQUIRY

Most County Archives and libraries hold a collection of local trade directories, as well as directories published for specialist occupations, and some of these can date back 200 years or more. These directories were originally produced for the bigger cities, but there's usually a good selection for smaller towns and counties. In the early ones, the names and addresses of many tradesmen are listed and, in the later ones, private householders were added. So let your fingers do the walking and try a bit of ancestor name spotting!

THE PROFESSIONALS!

If your ancestor was in one of the professions, look in a directory of its members or fellows. A directory published in the right time period will sometimes supply you with useful biographical info, such as academic training, how a member progressed in their career and even their addresses.

BIOGRAPHICAL BUMF!

You'd be surprised what turns up in the biographical section of the County Archives. Thousands of items, from personal letters, diaries and photographs to sales particulars, house deeds and family pedigrees are indexed by surname.

TO THE MANOR BORN...

Manorial records can go back to the 13th century, though, unfortunately, most of those before 1733 are written in Latin. Found in County Archives, the manorial rolls and books contain reports on the twice-yearly meetings of the Lord of the Manor or Court Baron and all the manor's ongoing shenanigans! Discover when tenants' land changed hands, where the land was situated, its size and annual rent. Other useful manorial records are the half-yearly rent books and rolls, which name tenants, their property and the rent due.

ANCESTORS BEHAVING BADLY

More serious crimes were heard by a Justice of the Peace at the Quarter Sessions. If one of your forebears committed a crime, there are various records you can consult at County Archives; these include things like:

- Rolls and papers – which give details of individual cases.

- Minute books.

- Lists of prisoners.

FOR LESS SERIOUS CRIMES...

Drunkenness and similar lapses weren't considered major crimes and were dealt with by the local magistrate at petty, county or borough sessions. Registers of the cases heard at these courts are now mostly held at County Archives.

I BEG YOUR PARDON!

Thousands of Britons left for the colonies – though not always willingly! After 1615, things began to look up for prisoners, and those who might once have been faced with a death sentence were often transported overseas instead. The National Archives hold a book by Peter Wilson Coldham called, *The Complete Book of Emigrants in Bondage, 1614-1775*, which gives a list of convicts transported during this time and where they were tried.

TRANSPORTATION

The National Archives hold registers of convicts transported to New South Wales and Van Diemen's Land (renamed Tasmania in 1856) from 1787 to 1870 and these are listed by ships' name and departure dates. The details include; prisoners' names, ages, the date and place of the trial, the offence committed and the length of the sentence.

JAIL HOUSE ROLL!

Jail calendars don't depict saucy shots of prisoners, but what they do reveal are interesting facts about those detained in the county lockup! Found in the County Archives, the calendars list:

- Names, ages and occupations of prisoners.

- The alleged crime.

- The verdict and sentence handed out.

WAS YOUR ANCESTOR ONE OF THE TWELVE GOOD MEN?

In 1825, only men aged between 21 and 60 could serve on a jury and lists of jurors can be found with Quarter Sessions records at County Archives. But they couldn't be just anyone; they needed to fulfill certain criteria. They had to have owned property worth at least £10 a year, leased property worth at least £20 a year or rented property worth at least £30 a year.

READ ALL ABOUT IT!

If you have the opportunity (and stacks of time to spare) then a library that serves your ancestor's district can be the best place for browsing copies of vintage newspapers for a reference to their death. My tip is to look for…

An obituary or death notice: These could supply you with added background information, such as who attended the funeral and who the closest relatives were. It might also help you identify other family connections by giving names and their relationship to the deceased.

Reports of sudden death: Stories of sudden deaths are often featured in local newspapers and might help solve a mystery for you. If one of your ancestors died young, it might have been the result of an accident and so is quite likely to have been reported on.

A CAREER IN THE ARMY?

If in the U.K., ask if your nearest reference library has a copy of the Army Lists if a member of your family was a commissioned officer in the British Army. The Lists were printed quarterly from 1879 to 1950 (and annually between 1754 and 1879) and can widen your knowledge of an ancestor's army career.

DID YOUR ANCESTORS MIGRATE TO BRITAIN?

The Aliens Act of 1793 meant that all foreigners arriving in Britain had to supply certain information to official bodies. Migrants already resident, and householders where they'd taken up lodgings, were required to give details of name, rank or occupation, and address to a local magistrate or a parish overseer and these declarations are likely to be held at County Archives.

LOST THE PLOT?

Luckily, records have been kept of where people are buried and these will provide you with names, dates and burial plot numbers. Once you have an idea of where your ancestor was buried, get in touch with the local council who'll have phone numbers for the municipal cemeteries in that area. County Archives will have contact details for individual churchwardens, if you think your ancestor was buried in a churchyard.

WRITTEN IN STONE…

… or not, as the case may be! Gravestones, especially older ones, have a nasty habit of becoming worn and illegible, but, with a lot of patience, you can often pick out enough of the wording to piece together some interesting data. The really clever tip here is to see if anyone has already done this laborious task for you. Family History Societies produce many useful booklets and CDs, including ones on monumental inscriptions.

TRACING ANCESTORS

Most County Archive offices have a photocopying rule or two. Usually a document that is too big, too fragile, or has a wax seal is a definite no-no. My tip is to take along a digital camera for photographing documents and some tracing paper for copying any relevant details from maps.

PHOTO FINISH

Do a trial run of your digital photographing techniques on some documents at home before attempting the real thing in the archives environment. Try your camera at different settings and at different distances from the document and check that the results are readable on screen and when printed out.

CHAPTER SUMMARY

- Some form of ID is required when visiting archive offices.

- Check archives' websites and online catalogs.

- Save time by ordering documents before you visit Kew.

- Look up your nearest Family History Centre.

- Professional and trade directories are valuable resources.

- Remember the County Archives' biographical section.

- Helpful documents are found amongst the Quarter Sessions records.

- Search newspapers for obituaries and death notices.

- Family History Societies publish monumental inscriptions.

- Practice taking digital photos of documents.

Widening
the Net

" *Search out the past… know yourself… look to the future.* **"**

Anon

Chapter 6

Widening the Net

With more and more genealogical data becoming available on the Internet, you might be in serious danger of info overload! So here are my top tips for using some of the best resources on the Web and what you might expect from them.

INTERNATIONAL GENEALOGICAL INDEX (IGI)

The IGI is a massive index of baptisms and marriages. This huge database, which contains more than 600 million names, is compiled by the Church of Jesus Christ of Latter Day Saints. The majority of entries on the index are taken from Anglican parish registers, with some taken from Baptist, Methodist and Independent registers but fewer from Quakers, Jews and Catholic sources.
www.familysearch.org

BUILDING BLOCKS

Give the IGI a shot if you don't know your ancestor's parish, as the entry will give you this information. Tracking someone down this way means you can now search the relevant parish registers for all those other family details. You'll be able to:

- Find where your ancestor was baptized (and probably born).

- Track them down if they moved from one place to another.

- Locate the parish where a couple married (usually where the woman lived).

COME OUT, WHEREVER YOU ARE!

You'd think that, somewhere amongst the millions of names listed on the IGI, they'd have the one you're looking for, wouldn't you? But don't be too surprised if your ancestor proves to be illusive because, although data has been used from every country, none of the indexes are actually complete. So use the IGI as a guide only.

WHEN THINGS DON'T ADD UP

The IGI is a terrific thing but, like a lot of resources, it does contain a number of discrepancies. This is because the indexes are a mixture of details taken from the primary sources and data supplied by private individuals and things don't always tally with what's found in the parish registers. So be sure to bear this in mind and always double-check the information you find in the IGI with that in the actual parish register.

THE ANCESTRY WEBSITE

Generally, the records are only accessible to subscribers, but there is usually a free trial period of a week or two. Here you can view the complete U.K. General Register Office indexes of births, marriages and deaths. The GRO resource is fully searchable, contains millions of names and covers the years from 1837 to 2005.

The England and Wales census data on Ancestry (1841 to 1901) shows images of the original records and can be viewed on a 'pay per view' or 'pay per voucher' system.

There's a free index for the 1881 England, Wales, Isle of Man and Channel Islands census. If you locate one of your ancestors, click on the 'view record' symbol to see all the other family members living at the same address – very helpful
www.ancestry.co.uk

DOCUMENTS ONLINE

This site gives you almost more family history documents than you can shake a stick at! Searching the digitized index won't cost you a penny, but there's a small charge to download an image. If you use this resource at The National Archives, viewing the images is free, but you pay for any copies you take.
www.nationalarchives.gov.uk/documentsonline

ACCESS TO ARCHIVES (A2A)

Not all the good stuff is held at The National Archives. Take a peek at the online catalog at A2A; this lists the whereabouts and reference numbers of millions of other records that are kept in local archive centers in England and Wales. Records cover dates from the 8th century to the present day.
www.nationalarchives.gov.uk/a2a

SCOTLAND'S PEOPLE

This is the official government source for Scottish genealogy. They have various charges to view the online documents, but there are almost 80 million of them! The site's data includes statutory registers (civil registration of births, marriages and deaths), old parish registers, wills and censuses.
www.scotlandspeople.gov.uk

MOVING HERE

The Moving Here website is a good one to try if you know your ancestors were immigrants to England during the last 200 years. Resources include documents, photographs and film clips. There's free access to an online catalog relating to those from the Caribbean, Ireland, South Asia and Jewish communities.
www.movinghere.org.uk

JEWISH GENEALOGICAL SOCIETY OF GREAT BRITAIN

The resources and databases here are useful for family historians who wish to trace their Jewish ancestors, whether they came to the U.K. from overseas or left for pastures new.
www.jgsgb.org.uk

FAMILY HISTORY SOCIETIES ONLINE

Family history societies aren't just an online resource, but it's much simpler to locate the online presence of any particular society by going through the Federation of Family History Societies website. The Federation's site has details of regional societies in England, Wales and Ireland listed alphabetically by county. Also included on their website are overseas societies in Australia, Canada, New Zealand and the U.S.A.
www.ffhs.org.uk

FAMILY HISTORY SOCIETIES AND LOCAL CONNECTIONS

Each individual family history society focuses on the genealogy of a specific region and it can be well worth signing up for membership in order to gain some insider know-how. Members collate heaps of local data, and these transcripts are available to other members or sold in booklets or on CD-ROM. The size and activity of family history societies vary, but their research databases include things like:

- Local surname lists.

- Various census indexes.

- Burial indexes.

- Some indexes to regional institutions.

- Monumental inscriptions.

- War memorials.

- Local police service records.

- Quarter Sessions.

GUILD OF ONE-NAME STUDIES

This is a U.K. based organization that welcomes new members. With over 8,000 surnames on their list, it's possible that someone has already taken the hard work out of researching your family name. Every one of the surnames is registered by a member who collects information worldwide and there's an easy to use search facility on their website.
www.one-name.org

CONTACT GUILD MEMBERS...

You don't need to be a member of the Guild of One-Name Studies yourself in order to contact its members. Guild members are under an obligation to answer any query, so long as you pay the postage.

- If you live in the same country as the member you wish to contact, send an S.A.E. with your query.

- If you live in a different country, you'll need to send 3 International Reply Coupons in lieu of stamps.

- If you contact them by email, you won't have to pay anything!

Not all of the Guild's members have their contact details displayed on the website but they are included on a printed register, which is available through the site.

WHAT TO ASK...

If you're contacting one of the Guild members, you'll get much better results if you can be specific about what you want to know. But don't overload them with information – sending your entire family history isn't a good idea!

1. Give details of the names you're looking into – the maiden name of a spouse can help distinguish someone with a common surname.

2. Provide any information you have regarding dates.

3. The location is important, so give details about any place your ancestors settled.

AND WHAT NOT TO ASK…

One-name studies can take years to put together and Guild members amass huge amounts of data. Their research is ongoing, with facts constantly awaiting validation, so the biggest no-no when approaching one of them is to ask them for 'everything you have on so and so'!

HISTORICAL DIRECTORIES

This is a handy website to visit if you want to look up your ancestor's professional career. Not all of the professions are listed, but you'll find those for:

- Some officers in the British Army.

- Dental surgery directory for 1925.

- Clergy list for 1896.

- Medical register for 1913.

www.findmypast.co.uk

A FAMILY BUSINESS…

The National Register of Archives has a website that is a database of details concerning family and business papers. The search facility allows you to explore by family or personal name, corporate name or place name and gives information about the dates and whereabouts of individual records www.nationalarchives.gov.uk/nra

HOSPITAL CORNER

With this database you can search for the location of specific hospital records in the U.K. Be warned though, most hospital records are subject to closure periods (often 100 years) and access to an individual's records is not normally allowed. My tip would be to talk to the archivist at the repository before you visit, to see what might actually be available to you. www.nationalarchives.gov.uk/hospitalrecords

BACK TO BASICS

Someone (probably) once said that a document was only as accurate as the person who transcribed it. Whenever possible, try to view the original data and avoid the scribes' version of Chinese Whispers! Lots of websites now have scanned copies of original documents posted online and this is the next best thing to seeing records in person.

NO PLACE LIKE HOME

If you have access to the Internet at home, do as much of your preliminary research as possible from the comfort of your own swivel chair. A lot of the background information you need to gather can be found online, thus enabling you to spend your time at the various archives studying the original sources that aren't available on the Web.

USING KEYWORDS

Searching for information on some genealogy websites is like looking for the proverbial needle in a haystack, with thousands of possible results throwing themselves at you. So, where the facility is offered, use the advanced or refined search boxes to narrow things down. These usually require a date range or location, or a keyword. But, as not all 'keywords' will be listed in the document index or catalog, you will end up with limited results. My tip is to search using name, date and location first, and then try various keywords if the search brings up too many results to trawl through.

AND FINALLY: HIRING A RESEARCHER

It's unlikely there'll ever be a time when all genealogical records are available online, so, sooner or later, you'll need to consult documents in the flesh. When it isn't feasible to do this yourself, hiring a researcher is the next best thing. Here are my tips for choosing the right researcher for you.

1. Website content varies but a researcher should willingly offer advice and be able to tell you what records are held in their local area.

2. Ask them for a recommendation from a previous client, though, understandably, many are reluctant to ask clients to give out their email addresses to strangers.

3. Get the researcher to do a small amount of work for you before sending larger sums of money.

Gin was one of the most popular drinks in the 17th century, and it's estimated that Britons were consuming 8,000,000 gallons a year.

CHAPTER SUMMARY

- Track down your ancestor's parish on the IGI.

- Remember that the IGI is not complete.

- The GRO indexes can be viewed on the Ancestry website.

- Locate the whereabouts of millions of documents at Access to Archives.

- Try the Moving Here website for immigrant ancestors to England.

- Find useful databases at Family History Societies.

- Trace your surname through the Guild of One-Name Studies.

- Try the National Register of Archives for family and business papers.

- Always view original documents whenever practicable.

- Do as much of your preliminary research from home as possible.

Poor Ancestors
– Rich Pickings

" Why waste your money looking up your family tree? Just go into politics and your opponents will do it for you! "

Mark Twain

Chapter 7
Poor Ancestors – Rich Pickings

Discovering you have a poor ancestor or two in your family tree could be to your advantage, even if it wasn't to theirs! Poor Law records are one of the richest sources available to family historians and can be found at the relevant County Archives.

Up until 1834, each parish was a self-governing body and accountable for its own poor. This meant that the wealthier folk of the parish paid money into the poor rate to help their less fortunate neighbors. This poor rate was collected and administered by the parish officers (overseers and churchwardens).

So, from apprentices to workhouses, here are my top tips for finding out how things really were!

THE OVERSEERS' ACCOUNTS

The detailed account books kept by the parish overseers are chock full of valuable information so should be near the top of your 'resources to search' list. The overseers' accounts date mostly from the 18th and 19th centuries and name those who were in need of poor relief, what was provided, and how much it cost. Here's a list of just some of those things:

- House rent – the amount and how often it was paid.

- Fuel.

- Essential clothing.

- Food.

- Ale.

- Medicines.

- Money paid to someone who nursed the sick.

- Coffins and shrouds.

SURVIVING THE HARD TIMES

You might still find something about your family in the Poor Law records, even if they weren't generally considered to be paupers. Ordinary families sometimes found themselves in reduced circumstances and unable to work due to injury or ill health.

LEGALLY SETTLED OR LEGAL SETTLEMENT?

Here's a confusing one! You'll find references to poor ancestors in the overseers' accounts about their place of legal settlement, which won't necessarily be the parish where they chose to live. Plenty of people lived in one parish but were required to seek aid from another.

SO WHAT IS THIS PLACE OF LEGAL SETTLEMENT?

From around 1662 to 1834, everyone had a place of legal settlement – though this could be different to their place of birth.

Legal settlement affected the poor particularly and here's why: Being responsible for their own people, the parish officers weren't too happy about supporting 'outsiders' so, if anyone looked like they might become a burden on the parish coffers, for whatever reason, they were often dispatched back to their own legal settlement pretty sharpish.

SETTLEMENT AND ILLEGITIMATE CHILDREN

Legitimate children automatically took their father's place of settlement, even if they were born somewhere else. But illegitimate children could claim a legal settlement in the place they were born. This led to many a pregnant girl being returned, post haste, to her own settlement!

REMOVAL ORDERS

These were the legal documents used to send someone back to their place of settlement. They often give helpful information about those being removed, including the names of spouses and dependent children.

DOWN ON THEIR LUCK

Another interesting set of papers, found amongst the Quarter Sessions cases, are those dealing with vagrancy. These examinations give name, age, parish of birth, and spouse's name. 'Vagrant' covered a multitude of situations and could be about any number of things:

- Women whose husbands had abandoned them.

- People who had become ill while journeying.

- Discharged soldiers and their families.

- Apprentices who had run away from cruel masters.

A MINUTE IN THE VESTRY!

If you've passed on the Vestry Minutes, believing they have rather less to do with family history than with the welfare of the vicar's vestments, think again! Each Easter, this was where the parish officers were elected and the yearly poor rate decided. Discussions regarding the parish poor were the main topic at these regular powwows, so take my tip and check them out.

INDENTURE ADVENTURE

Orphans and children of poorer families were often apprenticed. The masters were sometimes 'chosen' by the parish officers and weren't always any happier about the situation than the children! Two indentures were signed and one was handed to the apprentice when his apprenticeship was completed. If you find one of these indentures, it'll give you the following info:

Children in the
workhouse were
required to have
a minimum of
three hours
schooling a day.

- The name and age of the apprentice.

- The name of the apprentice's parents.

- The trade the apprentice learned.

- The apprentice's parish.

- The master's name and occupation.

YOUTH INITIATIVE!

An apprentice could be anything from 7 to 21 years old and some were undoubtedly used simply as a source of cheap labor. The overseers' accounts books might show a record of payment made to a local farmer or householder who'd taken a child in.

ILLEGITIMATE CHILDREN IN THE QUARTER SESSIONS RECORDS

If a couple didn't marry, a case against the putative father might be brought to the Quarter Sessions. These useful 'bastardy documents' will give you the father's name and place of residence. A good tip here: The Sessions are comprised of files and minute books – look for the relevant case in the minute books first and save heaps of time.

EXAMINATION AFTER BIRTH

A formal examination could be made after an illegitimate child was born. This was a sworn statement made by the mother before a Justice of the Peace and it reveals the father's name, place of residence and occupation, and shows whether the child was male or female.

BASTARDY BONDS

These were documents signed by fathers of illegitimate children, agreeing to a maintenance payment until the child was seven years old. They were used quite often in the 17th and 18th centuries to release the parish from financial responsibility. A Bastardy Bond relating to one of your ancestors will often give you the name of the man's father too, as it's likely he stood as one of the Bond's guarantors.

ANOTHER WAY TO DISCOVER A FATHER'S IDENTITY...

The overseer kept a careful tally of incomings and outgoings in his accounts book. This included payments made to mothers of illegitimate children and money collected from reputed fathers.

WORKHOUSE RULES

It wasn't compulsory to stay in the workhouse but, if a man left of his own accord, his family had to leave, too. Some admission and discharge registers are held in local archives and are a useful place to look if you think your ancestor may have spent some time in a workhouse. These registers give the names, ages, addresses, religion and dates of admission and discharge for each inmate.

FINDING ANCESTORS WHO DIED IN THE WORKHOUSE

When workhouse inmates died, their burials were often taken care of by family outside, and records of these are usually found in the family's parish church. When this didn't happen, the workhouse Board of Guardians arranged burial locally in unmarked graves, so search the parish register where the workhouse was situated, too.

AUCTIONING A PAUPER'S PROPERTY

Sometimes an overseer sold off a pauper's possessions in the hope of making back the money the parish had paid out in poor relief. Records of these sales may show up in the overseers' accounts or occasionally in the Quarter Sessions records.

CHAPTER SUMMARY

- Overseers' Accounts are full of valuable information.

- Many ordinary families claimed from the poor rate.

- At one time, everyone was assigned a 'place of legal settlement'.

- Removal orders often give details of whole families.

- The Vestry Minutes record useful poor law business.

- Apprentice indentures can offer further leads.

- Quarter Sessions' records may contain details of illegitimate children.

- An Examination after birth reveals details of an illegitimate child's father.

- Workhouse records are held at County Archives.

- Overseers sometimes sold a pauper's possessions in an auction.

Worldly Goods
and Chattels

" What the next generation will value most is not what we owned, but the evidence of who we were and the tales of how we loved. In the end, it's the family stories that are worth the storage. "

Ellen Goodman

Chapter 8
Worldly Goods and Chattels

While researching your family history, you might discover the last will and testament of a wealthy ancestor and this document can reveal all sorts of things about him. But it wasn't only wealthy people who made wills – even those with few belongings to leave often had strong opinions about who should get them!

There are plenty of hints you can pick up about your family's past from other documents, too. The following tips will help you learn more about your ancestors' property, possessions and standard of living.

WHERE THERE'S A WILL…

Before the civil probate registries came into being in 1858, wills were proved in church courts; the main ones in England and Wales being the Prerogative Court of York (PCY), which dealt with the northern dioceses, and the Prerogative Court of Canterbury (PCC), which dealt with the southern ones. These are the ones to check if your ancestor was reasonably well-heeled. But those with less to leave may have had their will proved in a lower court.

- Wills proved in the PCC from 1384 until 1858 are held at The National Archives.

- Wills proved in the PCY from 1389 until 1858 are held at the Borthwick Institute of Historical Research, York.

- Wills proved in lower courts are usually held in County Archives.

- Wills proved in the Welsh ecclesiastical courts from 1521 until 1858 are at the National Library of Wales, Aberystwyth.

- Scottish wills are held by the National Archive of Scotland.

FOR LATER WILLS…

It gets simpler (sort of). From the beginning of 1858, wills in England and Wales were proved either in the Principal Probate Registry at High Holborn, London, or at a District Probate Registry (full list on their website). There are indexes from 1858 to date at High Holborn, where you can also order document copies.
www.justice.gov.uk/courts/probate/family-history

The National Archives have copies of the annual indexes up to 1943 but if you live in, or are visiting, the relevant district, ask at the County Archives or reference library as most of them also have these indexes.

GET YOUR FREE WILLS INDEX HERE!

The registered copies of the Prerogative Court of Canterbury wills from 1384 to 1858 have been indexed and are available online. This is a particularly easy one to search and, for a small charge, will even take you to a digital image of the will.
www.nationalarchives.gov.uk/documentsonline

GRANT OF PROBATE

If you come across an ancestor's will, you'll find it consists of two documents – the will and the grant of probate. The will itself is usually considered to be the interesting bit, specifying how the testator's possessions should be doled out, but the probate grant can be very informative, too. Look out for a date, the executors' names and relationship to the deceased, and the value of the estate.

WILLING SUSPENSION!

If you have a burial date, you'll probably be thinking that it makes sense to use this as a starting point when searching for a will – and you'd be right. But wills weren't always proved within six months of a person's death, so you may need to search longer than you thought. Work forward from the burial date for up to 15 years.

WOMEN'S WILLS

Before the Married Women Property Act of 1882, women's possessions belonged to their husbands. This was not only a pretty raw deal but means wills made by married women are as rare as hen's teeth. But look for wills made by widows and spinsters because these can be revealing. If they had no children of their own, they probably left bequests to their own siblings, or to their nephews and nieces.

YOU'VE HAD YOUR SHARE!

Sometimes people distributed their worldly goods before they died; handing over property to a son or bestowing a marriage settlement on a daughter, for instance. If one of the deceased's children has been left a measly sum in a will – often a shilling – this token legacy usually indicates an earlier settlement for that child rather than a family fall out!

BUT WHO GOT HIS LAND?

There were two types of land ownership and two reasons why your ancestor's land might not be mentioned in his will. Any copyhold land was ultimately held by the manor and couldn't be transferred to another person without a lot of rigmarole and the say-so of the manorial court. Freehold land automatically passed to the nearest blood relative – with sons and male descendants first in line.

SCOTTISH WILLS

For wills of those north of the border, visit the Scotland's People website where you can search the indexes of more than 611,000 entries of wills and testaments (probate documents) from 1513-1901, free of charge. The index doesn't tell you the names of executors, trustees or heirs to the estate. Nor will you learn the deceased's date of death, or the value of the estate.

Scottish wills and testaments can give you the forename, surname, occupation and place of residence of the deceased, the court in which the testament was recorded, and the date. Two websites to check out:
www.scotlandspeople.gov.uk
www.nas.gov.uk

FOR LOYAL SERVICE...

Was one of your forebears a servant 'up at the big 'ouse'? If they were, the master – or mistress – might have mentioned them in his, or her, will. Loyalty was often rewarded with a small (sometimes very small) sum.

NEXT OF KIN PLEASE STEP FORWARD...

Even if your ancestor didn't leave a will, you may still be able to find something called a bond of administration (or admon). This was a legal document that gave the next of kin the authority to dispose of any property belonging to their late, lamented, nearest and dearest.

PERSONAL POSSESSIONS

A will usually mentions personal possessions only if these were left to someone specifically, but a probate inventory is often more revealing about your ancestor. An inventory will list their belongings, often room by room, and include stuff like furniture, tools, clothing, and so on.

After the Act of
1666, it was a legal
requirement that
all bodies be buried
wrapped in nothing
but woolen cloth.

INTESTACY AND WHO GOT WHAT…

When a man died without leaving a will, his personal estate was distributed according to a certain pecking-order.

1. His wife got one third.

2. His legitimate children got the rest, divided equally between them. They also got their mother's share if she was already dead.

3. Grandchildren got their parent's share, if that parent had died.

4. The deceased's parents.

5. The deceased's aunts and uncles (or their children).

A MARRIAGE SETTLEMENT

Some husbands presented their new brides with a settlement of money or property before the marriage took place. This legal document meant the lucky lady was entitled to a lifetime interest and could bequeath the money or property to her children in her will. The downside was that the Marriage Settlement often laid down rules of how much of her new-found wealth she'd be entitled to should she be widowed. Surviving Marriage Settlements are held in County Archives.

RENTAL RECORDS

If someone in your family line rented a property from an organization or a charity, the County Archives may well hold records of the tenancy. Chances are, you will already have a good idea of where they were living from searching the parish registers and census returns. The types of property you could look out for include:

- An almshouse.

- A school house.

- A parsonage.

- A railway cottage.

ESTATE PAPERS

The Estate account books of a local bigwig could give you some information about any property or land your forebear rented. These papers, often to be discovered in the County Archives, give names of all the estate tenants, what they were renting, and how much they paid.

GOOD DEEDS

Lots of old property deeds have survived, even if the buildings themselves have fallen down. A search in the County Archives, which covers the area in which your ancestor lived, could prove very useful in your family research. These deeds will indicate the location of the property your ancestor owned and will also give some details of its size. Whether your ancestor was buying or selling the property, other names will appear on the document and these could indicate other family members.

THE HEARTH TAX

Some people would tax anything! The one levied on hearths, at 2 shillings per hearth, was as unpopular as the rest, but, hey, the king had to live on something. Payable by the occupier rather than the owner of a property, those whose house was worth less than 20 shillings (£1) in annual rent were exempt. The Hearth Tax period was from 1662 to 1689, though not all records survive. They record both chargeable and non-chargeable households and are the nearest you'll get to a national census before the 19th century. The National Archives hold the originals, but many County Archives have transcripts.

LAND TAX RECORDS

This tax, with its annual listing of names, was brought in during the late 17th century, but, for family historians, the lists made between 1780 and 1832 could yield some interesting results. During these years, the Clerks of the Peace used the roll as a means of determining those who could vote in parliamentary elections. You'll find the Land Tax records mostly in County Archives, in the Quarter Sessions collections – they provide names of owners and tenants of houses and land, often with the names of the property given, too.

THE PARISH RATEPAYERS

People may have considered themselves fortunate to have money, but a lot less lucky when the rate bill dropped on the mat! The Churchwardens' Accounts gives a list of parishioners who contributed each year towards the poor rate, and the sum each paid.

TRY THE TITHE MAPS

A tithe was a payment made by parishioners to support the parish church and its clergy, and if your ancestor owned land, he would have handed over his tithe payment with the rest. Originally, this was a tenth of the yearly produce of the land and was paid in kind (wool, milk, crops, etc) but an Act in 1836 required that the payment be made in the form of a rent-charge. A survey of the whole of England and Wales took place and the tithe maps (held in County Archives) are the result, showing the boundaries of land and the acreage of fields.

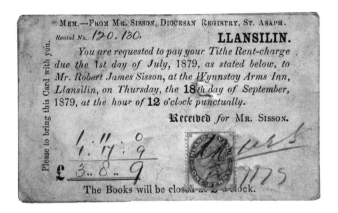

THE TITHE APPORTIONMENTS

The apportionments, with plot numbers matching those on the tithe maps, are the really useful half of the tithe double-act, and they supply all sorts of information:

- The name of the landowner.

- The occupier.

- The name of the property or land.

- The amount of rent-charge payable.

- The acreage.

- The state of cultivation: pasture, orchard, arable, garden, and so on.

CHAPTER SUMMARY

- A will might not have been proved for up to 15 years after a death.

- Look for a bond of administration if your ancestor didn't leave a will.

- Probate inventories are often more revealing than wills.

- Marriage settlements were quite common.

- Estate papers will list the names of tenants.

- The County Archives hold many property deeds.

- The Hearth Tax is the nearest thing to a pre-19th century census.

- Land Tax records provide names of owners and occupiers.

- Churchwardens' Accounts list those who contributed to the poor rate.

- Tithe apportionments give details about landowners and tenants.

Calendars and Dates and Spelling, Oh My!

" A man who thinks too much about his ancestors is like a potato – the best part of him is underground. "

Henry S. F. Cooper

Chapter 9

Calendars and Dates and Spelling, Oh My!

As if you didn't have enough to do, tracing all those ancestors back in time and deciphering all that undecipherable handwriting, you're now expected to learn a whole new language – well, almost. Once you set foot in the 1700s, you'll be sure to come across documents written in Latin, and you'll also need to take into account a calendar change. Use my tips for making sense of these records, and bluff your way out of trouble!

HOW TIMES CHANGE!

In England, under the old style Julian calendar, each year began on March 25th. But, by 1751, this calendar was incorrect by 11 days. Parliament decided England should keep up with the times (sorry!) and change to the new style Gregorian calendar (Scotland had already done this in 1660). Your ancestors' dates and ages might seem confusing if you don't allow for this changeover. Here's how it works:

1. The start of 1751 was on March 25th.

2. The year of 1751 ended on December 31st.

3. The new year of 1752 began on January 1st and ended December 31st.

4. In September of 1752, 11 days were taken out, so that September 2nd is directly followed by September 14th.

SHORT AND SWEET

In some of the older parish registers, the clergymen – to save all that arduous writing – recorded the names of months in a sort of shorthand: 8ber, 9ber, and so on. These will be referring to the pre-Gregorian calendar months, so 8ber is the old October and not the present day August.

THOSE ROMAN NUMERALS!

There were also quite a few clergy with a penchant for Roman numerals, which makes the early parish registers less than easy going. Make things easier for yourself by keeping a note of the basics and you'll never again be left scratching your head!

- M = 1000

- D = 500

- C = 100

- L = 50

- X = 10

- V = 5

- I = 1

So the year MDCCLXXXVIII = 1788

AND THOSE LATIN DATES!

A lot of the dates in older parish registers are written in Latin, but you might surprise yourself at just how many of these words you will recognize – or be able to make a shrewd stab at.

- On the first = primo

- On the second = secundo

- On the third = tertio

- On the fourth = quarto

- On the fifth = quinto

- On the sixth = sexton

- On the seventh = septimo

- On the eighth = octavo

- On the ninth = nono

- On the tenth = decimo

LATIN LINGO

Archivists are generally an obliging bunch, and there's usually at least one on duty at each County Archives office to help with those deciphering dilemmas! But, as with the Latin numbers, a lot of the words used – this time for baptisms, marriages and burials – will be instantly recognizable.

Baptisms: Look for similar words, like baptizat, baptizatus, baptizata or for words that sound like natal; renatus (reborn).

Marriages: Anything that looks like matrimony or nuptials is a safe bet; matrimonium or nupsit, for example.

Burials: This time look out for words similar to sepulcher or mortuary, such as sepultat or mortuus.

OH NO, MORE LATIN!

Hold on, I'm nearly done. Here are seven (almost) painless ways to sort out who's who:

1. Filia = daughter

2. Filius = son

3.   Uxor = wife

4.   Relicta = widow

5.   Vir = husband

6.   Mater/pater = mother/father

7.   Spurius = illegitimate

THE NAME GAME

After 1733, most clergy did us all a great favor and stopped using Latin in the parish registers. Here's a tip to ensure this good news doesn't present you with a brand new puzzle.

Your ancestor's forename, written down the Latin way for a baptism pre-1733 and later changed to the English spelling for a marriage or burial entry, might cause you to think you're dealing with two different people.

Some Latinized names later became popular names in their own right, but it's their English equivalent your ancestor would have been known by. Here're some popular ones:

- Maria – Mary

- Carolus – Charles

- Eliza – Elizabeth

- Gulielmus – William

- Jacobus – James

- Johanna – Joan

- Johannes – John

DECODING DE HANDWRITING

You're going to be coming across all kinds of handwriting, from the simple X to the ornate flourish with embellished twiddly bits. So here are three great interpreting tips:

1. The County Archives usually have books on handwriting styles covering various periods, or you can borrow one from your local library.

2. Use a magnifying glass and look closely at the handwriting you're trying to decipher. Pick out the letters, words and phrases you do recognize and compare these with the less legible ones.

3. I learned this trick some years ago. Take a sheet of plain paper and, using a pencil, copy the document you want to decipher, leaving spaces where you're unsure of a word or letter. As the document takes shape, many of the incomprehensible words become clear.

GRAVE MISTAKES

Be careful that the wording on an old tombstone doesn't trip you up. If you come upon a memorial where the inscription is clear enough to read, you might find it says something like 'Died in his 40th year'. This phrasing was commonly used, and means he hadn't yet reached 40, but died at 39.

WRITE THE DATES RIGHT!

Another thing you need to remember is that not everyone writes date figures in the same order, which means you may be wrongly recording vital information, especially from websites. In Britain, the standard practice is writing day-month-year, while in the U.S., for example, it's month-day-year, so 1-12-1850 could be either the 1st December, or January 12th.

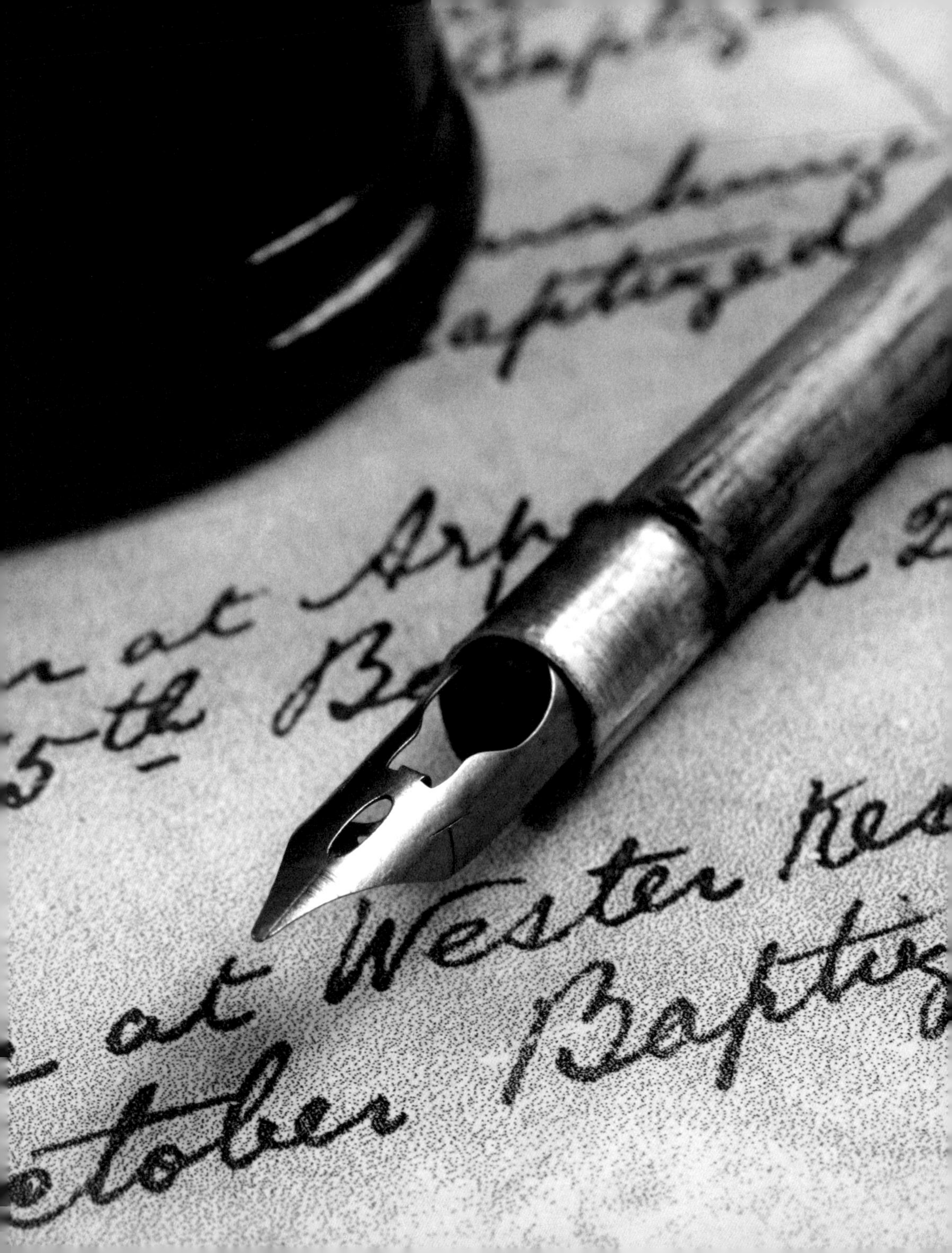

CHAPTER SUMMARY

- Latin documents are common in the 1700s and beyond.

- The start of a new year was once March 25th.

- There was a major calendar change in 1751-52.

- Watch out for the clergymen's Latin shorthand.

- Make a note of the basic Roman numerals.

- Many Latin words are easily identifiable.

- Learn to recognize the Latin equivalent of popular names.

- Pick up a book on different handwriting styles.

- Date phrasing on old headstones can trip you up.

- The order in which day-month-year is written can vary.

Thoroughly Modern Research!

" Nothing is so soothing to our self-esteem as to find our bad traits in our forebears. It seems to absolve us. "

Van Wyck Brooks

Chapter 10
Thoroughly Modern Research!

In genealogical terms, 'modern research' means anything less than a hundred years ago. But the time restrictions placed on a lot of modern records (often 50 or 100 years) means getting access to these documents can be very frustrating. Here are my top tips for researching some more recent family history.

FEEL FREE TO ASK

The Freedom of Information Act came into effect in 2005, which means you can wave goodbye to the old standard 30-year closure period on data held by public authorities. As you might expect, exceptions to this rule apply to records containing personally sensitive or confidential information, but this doesn't always mean an absolute closure. Under the Freedom of Information Act, you can request information from 'closed' records by writing to the head archivist in charge of the relevant repository.

SHOW OF HANDS

If you have a fairly good idea of your ancestor's address, you can take a look at the old electoral registers. In villages, these are listed by surname, but in towns they're entered by street name. The County Archives or local library will hold the electoral registers for their own district. So who was eligible to vote?

1. By 1900, men aged 21 and over.

2. From 1900, women who were the sole owners of a house and, therefore, ratepayers (but only in local elections).

Over a quarter of a million under-age boys enlisted before 1916. The minimum age was 18 (19 for service abroad).

3. After 1918, women over 30 or those who were university graduates.

4. After 1918, woman who owned businesses or were the wives of extensive householders.

5. After 1928, women over 21.

If your ancestor was getting any kind of help from the Poor Law system, they may have lost their vote.

IN THE CLUB!

You may not remember Granddad as the 'get up and go' type, but, in his sprightlier youth, he might have belonged to one of the many rambling or cycling clubs (an old group photo with Gramps sporting a pair of knobbly knees and a bicycle is a dead giveaway here). These sort of clubs were often very efficiently run, and records of members and their club activities may be available in the County Archives or reports of them may be found in local newspaper archives.

OTHER POPULAR PASTIMES…

Early 20th century newspapers are full of snippets about clubs and societies, which will give you an inkling of what folk did before TV was invented. Check out local archives for deposited records, which might include:

- A choral society.

- Dramatic society.

- Beekeepers.

- Photographic society.

- Automobile clubs.

- Angling associations.

- Bible society.

THE BRITISH RED CROSS SOCIETY

From 1910, county branches of the British Red Cross were set up in the whole of the U.K. If your ancestor was a member, County Archives may hold records, which could include membership information. Local newspapers will also have reported on branch activities.

WORKING ON THE RAILWAYS

A multitude of different railway companies existed before nationalization, employing many thousands of men and women – especially when the lines were being laid, and during the First World War. If a member of your family was once employed as a farm laborer, they may have been one of the many tempted away to work on local railway construction.

FOLLOW UP A LINE OF RESEARCH...

Keep track of your railway ancestor by consulting documents deposited in The National Archives (NA) by one of the rail companies. The NA online catalog will indicate if the specific records you're looking for are available. Content varies from one company to another but can include things like: name, age, job title, wage, and, occasionally, a full service history. During WWI, and before conscription in 1916, company registers recorded the names of men who were prepared to join up.

GETTING PERSONNEL!

If your forebear worked for the same firm over a long period, there could be a record of him in their personnel files. Businesses won't give out information about recent employees but might help with older records. And don't forget to ask County Archives and the local reference library – their ears might be worth bending when it comes to finding info about local firms.

NEWS FROM THE FRONT...

It can be profitable to search local newspapers covering the war years, especially if you know your ancestor was killed or badly wounded in action. Incidents involving local men were frequently reported on and can give details of the serviceman's regiment, his parents or wife, his address and his former place of employment.

UP CLOSE AND PERSONAL

Photographs of servicemen can be dated reasonably accurately, and taking a close look at the uniforms will be an aid in researching their service records. Using a magnifying glass, try to identify the badges, insignia and medals worn in the picture.

WAR GRAVES

The Commonwealth War Graves Commission has a database that lists the names of 1.7 million men and women of the Commonwealth forces who lost their lives in the two world wars. This 'Debt of Honour Register' is fully searchable online, and gives the cemetery or memorial where each individual is commemorated.
www.cwgc.org

CIVILIAN WAR CASUALTIES

If one of your ancestors was a civilian and a casualty of the Second World War, my tip is to search the Dept of Honour Register. This also gives information about the 67,000 civilians who were killed as a result of enemy action.

WWI CAMPAIGN MEDALS

Campaign medals were awarded to men and women who saw active service overseas. The Medal Rolls Index, brought into being towards the end of the First World War, lists details of medal entitlement, rank and unit

for all men and women who fought in the British Army or Royal Flying Corps. There's a free searchable database of the index at Documents Online, with a small charge to view the actual documents.
www.nationalarchives.gov.uk/documentsonline/medals.asp

A MENTION IN DESPATCHES…

The London Gazette published details of 'Honours and Awards' during both World Wars; the entries have been indexed and can be searched free online. Your search phrase will bring up entries that have that exact wording, so my tip is to try all variants – Frederick Smith, F. Smith, Smith F., and so on – you'll have your work cut out just searching 'Smith'!
www.london-gazette.co.uk/search

WOMEN'S ARMY AUXILIARY CORPS

Was your ancestor one of the 7,000 women who enrolled in the WAAC (1917-1918), later known as the Queen Mary's Army Auxiliary Corps (1918-1920)? There's lots of information to be had from the documents and enrolment forms:

- Name, address, age, and names and address of next of kin.

- Location, grade and promotions.

- ID certificate, references, casualty form, and uniform issued.

www.nationalarchives.gov.uk/documentsonline/waac.asp

REGIMENTAL MUSEUMS AND WEBSITES

A lot of regiments have their own museums, and many now have an online presence. The Imperial War Museum has an impressive collection of material on WWI and other conflicts involving Britain and the Commonwealth, from 1914 to the present day.
www.iwm.org.uk

WAR DIARIES

War diaries were kept by officers during WWI and some of these – arranged by battalion – are now online, with the digital images downloadable for a small fee.

www.nationalarchives.gov.uk/documentsonline/war-diaries.asp

BRITISH ARMY

The Long, Long Trail is another very useful website, with valuable data for family and military researchers, and contains info about the British Army in the First World War.

www.1914-1918.net

LOCAL DEFENSE RECORDS

Contact the County Archives for details of any military collections they hold. These might concern local militia, volunteer, territorial and home guard records.

LAND VALUATION

This involved a survey undertaken by the Inland Revenue around 1910; useful if your family were farmers or landowners. Those with less than 50 acres, and land worth less than £75 per acre, were exempt, and a hefty fine faced any landowner who failed to declare. The Valuation Books are held in County Archives and give the names and addresses of owners and occupiers, a brief description of the property, and a map reference.

SCHOOL REGISTERS

When a school closes, which frequently happens with village schools especially, the admission registers are often deposited at County Archives. Although there's usually a closure period, these records can be worth tracking down as they give details of:

- Pupil's name and date of birth.

- Names and address of parents or guardians.

- The names and date of birth of siblings.

- Date of admission to the school.

- Date and reason for leaving.

SCHOOL – THE BEST (OR WORST) DAYS OF THEIR LIVES!

Your ancestor's good (or not so good) conduct at school may have been recorded in the school log book. These logs were kept by the head teacher and recorded the school's curriculum, special achievements by pupils, and prizes awarded. More everyday happenings were also noted, including illnesses and punishments for bad behavior, or malingering and bunking off!

BACK TO SCHOOL…

School magazines often report on things like which pupils were awarded certificates on speech day, who won the cup on sports day, and who got the coveted leading role in the annual school production. Ask the school if such a magazine was ever produced – they may still have copies or someone could have deposited them in the County Archives.

THE ALIENS REGISTRATION ACT 1914

The Act affected those aged 16 or over who moved to the U.K. from overseas. The compulsory registration documents give name and address, age, marital status, race, occupation and employer. Surviving records can be found, either at County Archives, or a local police archive.

WE ARE SAILING…

You might find the names of emigrating ancestors from 1906 to 1951 on the ships' passenger lists held at The National Archives:

- Annual lists of ships departing from Southampton, Bristol and Weymouth up until 1908.

- After 1908, monthly lists from other ports.

- From 1921, daily lists from every port.

In was the custom in
Victorian times to cover
all the mirrors in the
house when someone died.

CHAPTER SUMMARY

- Records of clubs and societies are often deposited in local archives.

- The National Archives hold records of railway companies.

- Local businesses might have old personnel files.

- Newspapers frequently reported on local men injured in wartime.

- The Commonwealth War Graves Commission is a key resource.

- County Archives usually hold some military collections.

- Land Valuation Books give details of owners and occupiers.

- Many school records have been deposited with County Archives.

- School magazines can be very enlightening.

- The National Archives have ships' passenger lists for emigrants.

Create Your Own Family Archive

KEEPING NOTES

As filing systems go, clear plastic pockets in a ring binder are a hard arrangement to beat. With each plastic sleeve labeled, the information can be found quickly, and data added to and rearranged whenever you discover something new.

It's a nice idea to compile a separate 'profile' for each of your ancestors, adding new information about them as and when you find it. Include dates and places, along with all the relevant details of parents, birth or baptism, siblings, marriage, children, and death and burial. Then add in what you've unearthed about their home, their schooling, occupation or service history, and so on.

Always keep a record of the sources you've used: include the location, document title, index name, reference number, and date.

PRESERVING YOUR DOCUMENTS

Dirt, light, heat and moisture can all wreak havoc on your documents and photographs. Your family's history is worth preserving, considering the time, effort and money you've put into the project. Think of the data you collected, not just as your research notes, but as a family legacy you'll be passing on to future generations.

When handling your documents, be sure that everything, from your hands to the surface you are working on, is free from dust and grease. Archivists, who are handling old records on a regular basis, wear special thin, white cotton gloves. So, if you fancy kitting yourself out in a pair of these, they can be bought from suppliers of archival stationery.

PAPER

Sunlight and fluorescent lighting can cause paper to yellow and ink to fade, while damp encourages spotting and mould. Aim to store your documents in a dry place, which has a fairly constant temperature. Paper contains natural acids that can affect the document itself by seeping out over a period of time. Newsprint is especially acidic, and is also more prone to discoloring.

It's possible to buy acid-free folders to store records, and these will help prevent damage to individual documents as well as lowering the risk of papers contaminating each other. Clear plastic sleeves are best as they can be viewed without over-handling them.

Another good idea is to make copies of certain documents and use these for reference, while storing the originals in a safe place.

PHOTOS

Photographs are subject to all the same kind of environmental dangers as other documents – and then some.

Some photo albums may even damage your pictures over time, so keep your valuable prints in albums that are sold as 'archival quality', which means they're acid-free; or in special archive storage boxes, separating each photo with an acid-free sheet.

Copies of your old photographs should be done by a dedicated photo lab, rather than by the sort that offers an express developing service, as this really is a specialist job.

Scanning prints, or making photocopies of them, is a cheaper option and although the strong light of the copying machine won't do your pictures any favors, they will only be exposed to this for a very short time.

Precious photos should never be laminated, as this process can damage the print.

Useful Addresses

Borthwick Institute of Historical Research, University of York, Heslington, York YO10 5DD
Tel: 01904 321166 www.york.ac.uk/inst/bihr

Catholic National Library, St Michael's Abbey, Farnborough Road, Farnborough, Hants GU14 7NQ
Tel: 01252 543818 www.catholic-library.org.uk

College of Arms, Queen Victoria Street, London EC4V 4BT
Tel: 020 7248 2762 www.college-of-arms.gov.uk

Federation of Family History Societies, PO Box 8857, Lutterworth LE17 9BJ
www.ffhs.org.uk

General Register Office (England and Wales), Certificate Services Section, PO Box 2, Southport, Merseyside PR8 2JD
Tel: 0845 603 7788 www.gro.gov.uk

General Register Office (Ireland), Government Offices, Convent Road, Roscommon, Eire
Tel: 090 6632 900 www.groireland.ie

General Register Office (Northern Ireland), Oxford House, 49-55 Chichester Street, Belfast BT1 4HL
Tel 028 9151 3101 www.nidirect.gov.uk/gro

General Register Office (Scotland), New Register House, 3 West Register Street, Edinburgh EH1 3YT
Tel: 0131 334 0380 www.gro-scotland.gov.uk

The Institute of Heraldic and Genealogical Studies, 79-82 Northgate, Canterbury, Kent, CT1 1BA
Tel: 01227 768664 www.ihgs.ac.uk

Jewish Genealogical Society of Great Britain, 33 Seymour Place,
London W1H 5AU
Tel: 020 7724 4232 www.jgsgb.org.uk

Library and Archives Canada, 395 Wellington Street, Ottawa, Ontario,
Canada K1A 0N4
Tel: 1 866 578 7777 www.collectionscanada.gc.ca

National Archives (Australia), Queen Victoria Terrace, Parkes Act 2600,
Australia & PO Box 7426, Canberra Business Centre Act 2610, Australia
Tel: 1300 886 881 www.naa.gov.au

The National Archives (U.K.), Kew, Richmond, Surrey TW9 4DU
Tel: 020 8876 3444 www.nationalarchives.gov.uk

The National Archives and Records Administration (U.S.), 8601 Adelphi
Road, College Park, MD 20740-6001
Tel: 1 866 272 6272 www.archives.gov

National Archives of Ireland, Bishop Street, Dublin 8, Ireland
Tel: 003531 4072300 www.nationalarchives.ie

National Archives of Scotland, HM General Register House, 2 Princes Street,
Edinburgh EH1 3YY
Tel: 0131 535 1314 www.nas.gov.uk

National Library of Wales, Aberystwyth, Ceredigion, Wales SY23 3BU
Tel: 01970 632 800 www.llgc.org.uk

New South Wales State Records, PO Box 516, Kingswood,
NSW 2747 Australia
Tel: 02 9673 1788 www.records.nsw.gov.au

Principal Registry of the Family Division, Probate Searchroom,
First Avenue House, 42-49 High Holborn, London WC1V 6NP
Tel: 020 7947 7022 **www.justice.gov.uk/courts/probate**

Public Record Office of Northern Ireland, 2 Titanic Boulevard, Titanic
Quarter, Belfast BT3 9HQ
Tel: 028 90 534800 **www.proni.gov.uk**

Queensland State Archives, 435 Compton Road, Runcorn,
Queensland 4113
Tel: 7 3131 7777 **www.archives.qld.gov.au**

Religious Society of Friends Library, Friends House, 173-177 Euston Road,
London NW1 2BJ
Tel: 020 7663 1000 **www.quaker.org.uk**

Society of Genealogists, 14 Charterhouse Buildings, Goswell Road,
London EC1M 7BA
Tel: 020 7251 8799 **www.sog.org.uk**

State Record Office of Western Australia, Alexander Library Building, James
Street West Entrance, Perth Cultural Centre, Perth WA 6000
Tel: 08 9427 3360 **www.sro.wa.gov.au**

The Statue of Liberty-Ellis Island Foundation, INC. 17 Battery Place #210,
New York, NY 10004-3507
Tel: 212 561 4588 **www.ellisisland.org**

U.S. Citizenship and Immigration Services, 75 Lower Welden St,
Saint Albans, Vermont 05479 **www.uscis.gov**

Victoria Public Record Office, PO Box 2100, North Melbourne, VIC 3051
Tel: 3 9348 5600 **http://prov.vic.gov.au**

Index